The Reluctant Belligerent

❦ AMERICA IN CRISIS

A series of books on American Diplomatic History

EDITOR: *Robert A Divine*

The Reluctant Belligerent:

AMERICAN ENTRY INTO WORLD WAR II

Second Edition

ROBERT A. DIVINE
The University of Texas
Austin, Texas

McGraw-Hill, Inc.
New York St. Louis San Francisco Auckland Bogotá
Caracas Lisbon London Mdrid Mexico Milan
Montreal New Delhi Paris San Juan Singapore
Sydney Tokyo Toronto

THE RELUCTANT BELLIGERENT

Second Edition

19 20 21 22 23 24 25 QSRQSR 9 8 7 6 5 4 3 2

Library of Congress Cataloging in Publication Data:

Divine, Robert A
    The reluctant belligerent

    (America in crisis)
    Bibliography: p.
    Includes index.
    1. World War, 1939–1945—United States.
2. United States—Foreign relations—1933–1945.
3. World War, 1939–1945—Causes. I. Title.
II. Series

D753.D57   1979   940.53'73   79-11460
ISBN 0-07-554672-8

To the memory of John F. Kennedy

Foreword

"THE UNITED STATES always wins the war and loses the peace," runs a persistent popular complaint. Neither part of the statement is accurate. The United States barely escaped the War of 1812 with its territory intact, and in Korea in the 1950s the nation was forced to settle for a stalemate on the battlefield. At Paris in 1782, and again in 1898, American negotiators drove hard bargains to win notable diplomatic victories. Yet the myth persists, along with the equally erroneous American belief that we are a peaceful people. Our history is studded with conflict and violence. From the Revolution to the Cold War, Americans have been willing to fight for their interests, their beliefs, and their ambitions. The United States has gone to war for many objectives — for independence in 1775, for honor and trade in 1812, for territory in 1846, for humanity and empire in 1898, for neutral rights in 1917, and for national security in 1941. Since 1945 the nation has been engaged in a long struggle to contain communism and defend the democratic way of life.

The purpose of this series is to examine in detail the critical periods relating to American involvement in foreign war from the Revolution through Vietnam. Each author has set out to recount anew the breakdown of diplomacy that led to war and the subsequent quest for peace. The emphasis is on foreign policy, and no effort is made to chronicle the military participation of the United States in these wars. Instead the authors focus on the day-by-day conduct of diplomacy to explain why the nation went to war and to show how peace was restored. Each volume is a synthesis combining the research of other historians with new insights to provide a fresh interpretation of a critical period in American diplomatic history. It is hoped

that this series will help dispel the illusion of national inno-
cence and give Americans a better appreciation of their country's role in war and peace.

ROBERT A. DIVINE

Preface to the Second Edition

I N PREPARING A NEW EDITION OF THIS BOOK, I have drawn on the important new work on this topic done by historians in recent years. While retaining most of the material from the first edition, I have made many changes and additions designed to reflect this recent scholarship. I am grateful to Kinley J. Brauer, Richard T. Ortquist, and David M. Pletcher for suggesting needed areas for revision and to Walter LaFeber for pointing out important new material from the British records on the Atlantic Conference. My debt to the many historians who have written since 1965 on American foreign policy in the 1930s is indicated in the expanded bibliographical essay.

I have also altered the tone and softened the wording of interpretive passages in order to reflect my own shifting perspective on the crisis of the 1930s and the way the United States responded to it. The Vietnam experience has made me more understanding of the isolationist position and less dogmatic about the refusal of Franklin D. Roosevelt to take vigorous steps to meet the Axis threat. I still believe, however, that the passive nature of American foreign policy in the 1930s contributed to the coming of World War II. Faced with the aggressive challenge posed by Germany and Japan, the United States refused to play its rightful role of world leader and instead retreated behind the facade of neutrality legislation. Early and sustained American support of the existing balance of power in the world might well have helped England, France, and China contain the expansive thrust of the Axis nations and spared the globe the agony of World War II. Instead the American people and their leaders, fearful of involvement in another terrible war, tried to insulate themselves from the conflict. This effort at escape proved unavailing; the German victories in Europe and Japanese expansion in Asia finally forced the United States to adopt active policies of resistance that led inevitably to American entry into World War II. In the pages that follow, I try to demonstrate how this failure of leadership jeopardized the nation's security and added to the severity of the Second World War.

ROBERT A. DIVINE

Contents

MAPS

(All maps by Theodore R. Miller)

CHAPTER 1

The Innocent Bystander

". . . THE ONLY THING we have to fear is fear itself," declared
Franklin D. Roosevelt in his first inaugural address on March
4, 1933. The fear that the new President sought to assuage was
a very real one. That morning the governors of New York and
Illinois had closed the banks in their states, and the country's
financial life virtually ceased. The nation was at the moment
of deepest crisis in the great depression, and the American
people waited anxiously for Roosevelt to take decisive action.
Focusing on the domestic emergency, the President barely
mentioned foreign affairs in his speech. "In the field of world
policy I would dedicate this Nation to the policy of the good
neighbor—the neighbor who resolutely respects himself and,
because he does so, respects the rights of others."[1] Thus, with
one generality, Roosevelt dismissed his country's role in world
affairs.

Eight years later, fear again spread through the United
States. German armies had swept over Europe, driving France
into lightning defeat and forcing the British off the Continent.
In the summer of 1941, Nazi forces were advancing on Leningrad and Moscow, and military commentators were predicting
the fall of Russia by the end of the year. The threat in the Far
East was even more awesome. Japan had gained control of the
most valuable provinces of China and was moving into Southeast Asia, threatening the British in Malaya, the Dutch in the
East Indies, and the American outpost of the Philippines. At
home, Roosevelt had carried out his New Deal program, but

[1]Samuel Rosenman, ed., *The Public Papers and Addresses of Franklin D.
Roosevelt* (13 vols.; New York, 1938-1950), II, 11, 14.

now both he and the American people had to face a new challenge. The "good neighbor" phrase of the 1930s, made meaningful in Latin American policy, resounded irrationally in a world of bad neighbors who threatened the security of the United States. The challenge of aggression was a fact most Americans learned slowly in the depression decade. But their teachers, Hitler, Mussolini, and the Japanese militarists, provided the dramatic instruction that gradually destroyed the isolationist mood of the 1930s and led to American entry into the Second World War.

I

When the new administration took office in the early spring of 1933 many observers believed that it would make sweeping changes in American foreign policy. Under the Republican Presidents of the 1920s, the United states had held itself aloof from the world, engaging in many diplomatic conferences, tightening the stranglehold on the world's economy the nation had achieved during the First World War, but refusing to take responsibility for the peace of the world. After rejection of the Treaty of Versailles and the League of Nations by the Senate in 1919-20, the United States dedicated itself to a nationalistic foreign policy. Tariffs were raised, payment of war debts demanded, and political guarantees and commitments adamantly avoided. Taking as their motto, what is good for the United States is good for the world, the American people supported a foreign policy of self-indulgence that reflected the hedonistic mood of the 1920s. When challenged by foreign critics, Americans could point to the Kellogg-Briand Pact — the treaty which outlawed war except in self-defense.

The election of Franklin D. Roosevelt marked the return to power of the party of Woodrow Wilson, and thus seemed to promise a break with the nationalism of the 1920s. Roosevelt had been a loyal Wilsonian, serving as Assistant Secretary of the Navy and later running as Vice-Presidential candidate in 1920 on a pro-League platform. In the 1920s Roosevelt continued to champion the League and internationalism, playing a leading role in the creation of the Woodrow Wilson Foundation, which sought to perpetuate Wilson's ideals in foreign policy. As an aspiring politician, he gradually shifted with the prevailing nationalist sentiment. In 1922 he wrote his former running mate, James Cox, "I am not wholly convinced that the country is quite ready for a definite stand on our part in favor of immediate entry into the League of Nations."[2] Later in the decade, when he was developing more serious ambitions for the White House, Roosevelt wrote an article for the periodical *Foreign Affairs* in which he endorsed the principle of international cooperation in glowing terms but carefully avoided making any specific commitments. In 1932 political expediency led Roosevelt to repudiate the League of Nations; he stated that it was no longer the organization that Wilson had struggled to achieve.

Despite Roosevelt's drift away from internationalism, those who hoped to resurrect the Wilsonian ideals rejoiced at his election. They were encouraged by the selection of Cordell Hull as Secretary of State. Hull, a Tennessee Senator who had served in the House during the Wilson years, was a dedicated exponent of international cooperation, particularly the liberalization of trade barriers. Endowed with a salty vocabulary, a rigid code of honor, and a gift for political infighting which enabled him to survive for eleven years in the Roosevelt cabinet, Hull viewed world issues in terms of moral principles. To Hull diplomacy was the art of preaching, not of negotiation. His closest confidant and adviser was Norman H. Davis, a fellow Tennessean who had made a fortune in Cuban sugar and banking. Davis had served as a financial adviser to Wilson at Paris, but had been passed over for the post of Secretary of State by Roosevelt because of his close association with the House of Morgan. He possessed the skill at diplomatic bargaining which Hull lacked, and he was a fervent believer in collective security.

The State Department was slanted toward internationalism, but there were some strong balances. Raymond Moley, the Co-

---

[2]Frank Freidel, *Franklin D. Roosevelt: The Ordeal* (Boston, 1954), p. 122.

lumbia professor who had organized Roosevelt's "brain trust" during the 1932 campaign, became an Assistant Secretary of State much to the disgust of Hull. Moley was an intense economic nationalist who believed that the depression must be beaten at home by government action which would preclude any effort at international currency stabilization or tariff reduction. Moley's views were shared by many key New Dealers in other departments of the government, and the more general belief that foreign policy must play a secondary role until the domestic crisis was eased pervaded the Roosevelt administration. The strength of this sentiment became apparent in June 1933 when Roosevelt, going even beyond Moley's position, undermined the World Economic Conference at London by refusing to agree to currency stabilization. On the economic front the United States was pledged to a nationalist effort to overcome the depression without regard to the rest of the world. The following year Roosevelt finally did accept Hull's proposal for reciprocal tariff reduction, but though many such treaties were signed in the 1930s, the breakdown of world trade had progressed so far in the depression years that little advance was made toward restoring an international economy.

The most serious diplomatic problems facing the new administration came in the Far East. Japan had succeeded in destroying the American Open Door Policy by her conquest of Manchuria in 1931 and 1932. Although Secretary of State Henry L. Stimson protested vigorously against the Japanese aggression, President Herbert Hoover refused to permit any policy stronger than moral disapproval in support of China. Stimson had finally resorted to the device of nonrecognition, informing both China and Japan on January 7, 1932, that the United States could not recognize as legal any infringement of American commercial rights in China or the violation of the administrative and territorial integrity of China. The League of Nations eventually supported this nonrecognition policy, but Japan ignored it, establishing the puppet state of Manchukuo in the spring of 1932 and finally withdrawing from the League of Nations. Although Stimson's moral sanctions had little effect, he was successful in persuading President-elect Roosevelt to continue the policy of non-recognition of Japanese aggression. Many isolationists feared that Roosevelt would embark on a new crusade against the Japanese, but with the United states preoccupied with the depression and Japan intent on consolidating her gains in Manchuria, the Far Eastern situation eased. Yet, significantly, Roosevelt and Hull were committed to oppose further Japanese aggression in Asia.

The problems of Europe in 1933 were at once less critical and more complex than those of the Far East. The Versailles settlement had left England and France in uneasy control of the European balance of power. Germany had been disarmed by the treaty, and during the early 1920s she had been crippled by inflation. The problem of Germany was one of political stability and economic vitality—potentially the wealthiest and most powerful nation on the continent, her difficulties troubled the victors in the First World War. In the early twenties Germany had turned to the Soviet Union, ignored and rejected by England and France, and the two had agreed at Rapallo on a cautious alignment. The alarmed Western powers had responded by efforts to strengthen the League, and when these failed, they tried traditional diplomacy. At Locarno in 1925, Britain and Italy guaranteed an agreement between Germany, France, and Belgium to respect their common frontiers in the West. In 1926 Germany was admitted to the League of Nations. Although the issue of reparations continued, the major German grievance was disarmament. Under the terms of the Treaty of Versailles, Germany was stripped of her navy and compelled to limit her army to 100,000 men. The victorious powers had pledged themselves to secure general arms limitation in accordance with Wilson's fourth point, but had never done so. When Germany insistently raised the cry of equality in armaments, Britain and France took the preliminary steps toward convening an international disarmament conference at Geneva. After repeated delays the conference opened on February 2, 1932, with an American delegation in attendance.

The disarmament conference moved slowly toward ultimate collapse. Germany demanded equality in arms; France insisted that she could not agree to disarmament without political guarantees for her security. The Soviets called for general and unlimited disarmament, while Britain and the United States advocated limiting "offensive" weapons. When Roosevelt became President, he appointed Norman Davis to head the American delegation. In March 1933 Roosevelt, Hull, and Davis held a series of conferences before Davis left for Geneva. French fear of a rearmed Germany was the great obstacle to agreement, and Davis searched for a way to give France some guarantee of assistance in case of attack by Germany which would be acceptable to Congress. In April Davis cabled home that the United States offer to surrender its traditional neutral rights and agree not to trade with an aggressor in a European conflict. The State Department quickly concurred, and in late April President Roosevelt gave his consent. The State Department was already sponsoring a resolution in Congress, which had originated under Stimson in the Hoover administration, that would permit the President to embargo the export of arms to any country he designated. The House passed this resolution in mid-April, and the administration pressed for Senate approval in order to implement the policy Davis had suggested.

Davis offered the new American proposal to the disarmament conference on May 22, 1933. He told the delegates that if a successful disarmament agreement were achieved, the United States would pledge to meet with other nations when there was a threat to world peace, and if it agreed that one nation was guilty of aggression, "we will refrain from any action tending to defeat such collective effort which these states may thus make to restore peace."[3] Under Davis' pledge, though the United States would not join in economic sanctions against an aggressor, it would adjust its policy to avoid defeating measures of collective security adopted by other nations. This was the most advanced position that any official American spokesman had taken on a major issue of world politics since 1919.

Two days later, on May 24, the Senate Foreign Relations Committee met to consider the House resolution which would

[3]Department of State, *Peace and War: United States Foreign Policy, 1931–1941* (Washington, 1943), pp. 188-189.

make the Davis pledge effective. The chairman, Senator Key Pittman of Nevada, best noted for his fondness for silver, liquor, and profanity, cared little for the new departure of the administration, and his committee was dominated by two staunch isolationists, William E. Borah of Idaho and Hiram Johnson of California. Both were Republicans and leaders of the irreconcilables of 1919. Johnson was highly suspicious of the arms embargo resolution, and he insisted that it be amended to apply impartially to all belligerents in any war. Johnson's amendment was designed to change a collective security proposal into an isolationist one, for instead of denying arms to the aggressor, by its terms the President would be compelled to play a weak role, banning arms to the innocent as well as the guilty. Nonetheless, when Pittman confronted Roosevelt with this situation on May 25, the President agreed to accept the Johnson amendment, thereby destroying the policy Davis had announced at Geneva only three days before. An outraged Cordell Hull finally prevailed upon Roosevelt to kill the entire arms embargo resolution in Congress, but the damage had been done. Roosevelt had given way on a major effort to reorient American foreign policy at the first sign of isolationist opposition. There was gloom in the State Department, but among the isolationists on Capitol Hill, there was only eagerness to move on from this first victory. As Roosevelt, caught in the midst of domestic crisis, defaulted in his role of leader in foreign policy, Congressional isolationists moved to take his place.

II

The fate of the arms embargo resolution in the Senate revealed the strength of the isolationist leaders in Congress. Johnson and Borah dominated the Foreign Relations Committee. Both were western Progressives who shared the intense nationalism of Teddy Roosevelt without possessing the Republican Roosevelt's broader understanding of world affairs. Although Borah had supported the Kellogg-Briand Pact, his record in foreign affairs was negative; he found a flaw in nearly every proposal and treaty, and his few constructive services came in opposing State Department policies on foreign loans and nonrecognition of the Soviet Union. Johnson was even more negative and narrowly vindictive in his view of the world. His single legislative contribution to American foreign policy in more than two decades was the Johnson Act, forbidding private loans to foreign governments in default on their war debt. Johnson and Borah were bitterly suspicious of the British, and they insisted that the United States go its own way in the world, aligning itself with no other nation and defending its own interests, by war if necessary, entirely on its own.

In contrast, many of the other Congressional isolationists abhorred the use of force and favored isolationist policies to avoid involvement in foriegn wars. Many who shared the Progressive tradition, notably Senators Robert La Follette, Jr., George Norris, and Gerald P. Nye, reacted against the nationalism of Borah and Johnson; they saw economic forces and special interests as the instigators of war. Norris and La Follette's father had voted against war in 1917, charging that selfish economic interests were behind the conflict, and Nye, although he favored war in 1917, came to share this viewpoint by the 1930s. All three men represented the Middle West, with its ethnic ties to Germany, its interior geographic location, and its agrarian economy—factors which historians have identified with isolationism. Above all, these men viewed the depression as a long-range result of the First World War, and they attributed the causes of that war to greedy manufacturers and bankers who had sought to profit from the wartime trade with the Allies. They were determined to do all they could to prevent future wars and the economic breakdowns that followed.

The distinguishing feature of the isolationism that prevailed in the United States in the 1930s was its variety. Isolationists ranged broadly across the political spectrum, from liberal-minded reformers like Norris to such entrenched conservatives as Herbert Hoover and Robert A. Taft. Although isolationism was often identified with the Middle West, many of its staunchest advocates came from other regions, such as Hiram Johnson of California and Representative Hamilton Fish of New York.

Politically, Republicans predominated, but such influential Democrats as Senator Burton Wheeler of Montana and Bennett Clark of Missouri voiced strong isolationist views. Unilateralism — the belief that the United States should go it alone in world affairs, free from alliances or commitments to other nations — was the unifying thread, together with a fear of war. Two developments in the 1930s intensified the isolationist mood. The first was the great depression, which turned national attention inward. The American people became so preoccupied with the problems of unemployment and economic paralysis that they had little interest in the world beyond their borders. And then the rising threat of aggression overseas, beginning with the Japanese conquest of Manchuria in 1931 and reaching its climax with Adolf Hitler's bellicose acts later in the decade, reinforced the desire to stay aloof from an increasingly dangerous world situation.[4]

Outside Congress there was a strong pacifist movement which had gained strength all through the 1920s. Many of the older, conservative peace societies, such as the American Peace Society, the World Peace Foundation, and the Carnegie Endowment for International Peace, continued their educational work, supporting the League of Nations as the best hope for mankind. A large number of more radical pacifist societies had sprung up during and after the First World War. Uncompromising in their aims, they condemned the League because it relied ultimately on force through economic and military sanctions to preserve world peace. Demanding total disarmament as the only way to abolish war, such groups as the National Society for the Prevention of War and the Women's International League for Peace and Freedom sent observers to disarmament conferences, hired lobbyists to appear before Congressional committees, and organized American women and the churches in their cause.

In the early 1930s the failure of the disarmament conferences led the pacifist leaders to search for villains. They found them among the industrialists and financiers who con-

[4]Manfred Jonas, *Isolationism in America, 1935–1941* (Ithaca, New York, 1966), pp. 15-26.

trolled the munitions industry. A series of books and magazine articles appeared in 1933 and 1934 dealing with the "blood brotherhood," the international ring of arms makers who were accused of fomenting wars, sabotaging disarmament, and inciting arms races. With the spotlight focused on the munitions makers, Miss Dorothy Detzer, the skillful and persuasive lobbyist for the Women's International League, believed it was time to press for a Congressional investigation of the arms trade, which she hoped would lead to the nationalization of the munitions industry. She approached Senator George Norris, who strongly approved her idea, and together they went down the roster of the Senate to select the man to conduct the probe. Ruling out senator after senator, they finally had one name left — Gerald P. Nye of North Dakota. With Norris' help, Miss Detzer succeeded in persuading Nye to introduce a resolution calling for a Senate investigation of the arms trade. As a result of some shrewd parliamentary maneuvering, Nye won approval for his committee, and when Vice-President Garner allowed the committee to name its own chairman, the group surprised the administration by selecting the Republican Nye.

The Nye committee began its public hearings in September, 1934. All summer long a group of investigators had pored through the records of such firms as the Du Pont Company, Remington Arms, and Bethlehem Steel, and had subpoenaed thousands of letters, confidential agreements, and legal memorandums. When the executives of these corporations testified before the committee, they were asked to explain the conduct of their firms. But the committee was interested in exposure, not explanation. The testimony and the official exhibits, which covered the years 1914 to 1934, revealed many unsavory details of the arms trade — the huge profits of munitions makers in the war, the close connections of the arms makers with the War and Navy Departments, the unscrupulous sales techniques used to export arms to Latin America and China. Outside the hearing room Nye made speeches suggesting that American entry into the war was based solely on economic factors. The records of the committee hearings did not substantiate this indictment, but the bold headlines and the dramatic charges that appeared day after day in the daily press brought this message home to the American people.

Walter Millis, a young editorial writer for the New York *Herald Tribune*, reinforced the Nye thesis with his popular historical account, *Road to War: America, 1914-1917*. Although Millis avoided the crude economic charges that Nye made, he showed that American policy from 1914 to 1917 allowed the Allies to develop a huge and increasingly indispensable war trade with the United States that was closed to Germany. Calling the United States "a silent partner of the Entente," Millis leveled his sharpest barbs at Colonel House, who he felt misled Wilson into such an unneutral policy.[5] Millis never reached any specific conclusion, but his book, which became a Book-of-the-Month selection, left the indelible impression that American entry into the World War had been a tragic mistake.

While the isolationists developed their economic theories over American entry into the First World War, they met determined opposition from a small but highly articulate band of internationalists. Although the oratory of Woodrow Wilson had failed to sway the Senate in 1919, this great idealist had won the support of a large number of men for his concept of collective security.

In 1922, a group of staunch Wilsonians met in New York City to found the League of Nations Non-Partisan Association. Centered in the East, the new organization lobbied strenuously in 1924 to get the Democrats and the Republicans to support entry into the League of Nations in their party platforms. When this effort failed, the Association shifted to a drive to gain American membership on the World Court. This judicial body, separate from the League of Nations, consisted of an impartial panel of judges to arbitrate international disputes voluntarily submitted to it. Yet even this modest form of international association failed when the Senate added a reservation that proved unacceptable to the other member nations.

While the League of Nations Association spent its energies on lost causes in the 1920s, two other groups emerged with the broader goal of educating the American people on world affairs. The Council on Foreign Relations, formed in New York City in 1921, consisted of businessmen with international in-

---

[5]Walter Mills, *Road to War: America, 1914-1917* (Boston, 1935), p. 89.

terests, scholarly experts on foreign policy, and officials from the State and Treasury departments. Adopting an elitist approach, the Council published the distinguished periodical *Foreign Affairs* and brought together regularly the leaders of business and finance with academic and government specialists. The Foreign Policy Association, in contrast, tried to reach a broader segment of the American people. Founded by such liberal intellectuals as Charles A. Beard and Herbert Croly, the Foreign Policy Association sent out a weekly digest on world affairs to newspaper editors across the country and published a variety of pamphlets and brochures designed to make the general public internationally conscious and aware of American responsibility for peace.

In the 1930s the internationalists, despite repeated setbacks and frustrations, appeared to grow in strength as world events bore out their prophecies. In the previous decade their warnings of eventual war unless all nations united in collective security seemed unreal. With the Manchurian crisis and the advent of Hitler, internationalists spoke with new vigor, confident that they had the only sane solution to world problems. They renewed their pleas for American membership on the World Court, and finally in January 1935 the Senate again debated this question. To the dismay of the internationalists, an avalanche of last-minute letters and telegrams stirred up by Father Coughlin and the Hearst press resulted in the defeat of the World Court protocol by seven votes in the Senate. Internationalism was still a minority view.

III

Most Americans in the 1930s were neither isolationists nor internationalists. Rather than adhering to any dogmatic views of foreign policy, they simply ignored the world. They no longer had any specific goals in their foreign policy beyond the naive desire to live and let live. The sense of mission which had powered America's rise to world power had burnt itself out in Wilson's great crusade, and most Americans were content to drift. This indifference meant that American foreign policy

would be framed not in Washington but in foreign capitals—
in London and Paris, in Moscow and Rome, and mainly in
Berlin and Tokyo. With the President deeply involved in overcoming the depression, Congress dominated by isolationists,
and the people apathetic toward international affairs, the
United States played the role of innocent bystander as the
world edged slowly toward war.

CHAPTER II

Neutrality

THE PATTERN of American policy in the 1930s—foreign action, American reaction—emerged with the disintegration of the Versailles settlement. When Hitler reached power in 1933, his avowed goal was to revise the Treaty of Versailles and restore Germany to its "rightful" place in Europe. Americans disliked Hitler and had no sympathy for his National Socialist movement, which endorsed purges, concentration camps, and violent anti-Semitism. But few Americans realized that Hitler's basic objectives would nullify the results of the First World War and jeopardize the nation's security. The dispatches of American foreign service officers in Berlin repeatedly warned that Hitler was bent on eventual world domination, but their prophecies remained buried in State Department files.

At first, Hitler moved cautiously in foreign affairs, participating in the disarmament conference at Geneva, clothing his desire for rearmament with the diplomatic demand for equality. When the French stubbornly resisted Hitler's requests, Germany abruptly withdrew from the conference and from the League of Nations in October 1933. This bold act, which went unchallenged, signified Hitler's determination to upset the status quo. He scored a stunning diplomatic victory three months later when he signed a nonaggression pact with Poland, which protected Germany from the traditional danger of a two-front war. When the disarmament conference met again in the spring of 1934, Germany's absence proved fatal, and the major European powers abandoned the conference for bilateral negotiations with Germany on the arms question. The lack of determination by England and France encouraged Hitler, and on March 10 he permitted Marshal Goering to announce that Germany had secretly established a substantial air force in violation of the treaty of Versailles. Six days later Hitler openly denounced the disarmament clauses of the treaty, and stated that Germany would reinstate universal conscription. To the amazement of the world, the German dictator declared that he intended to maintain an army of 550,000 men, twice as many as he had sought in negotiations with Britain and France.

Hitler's rearmament proclamation led to a brief show of unity by the victors of World War I — Britain, France, and Italy. Meeting in Stresa in April 1935, the two prime ministers joined Mussolini in resolving to maintain the existing treaty structure of Europe and to resist any attempt to change it by force. The leaders then prevailed on the League Council to condemn German violation of the Treaty of Versailles by a unanimous vote. But when Britain, France, and Italy failed to back their words with any effective action, Hitler knew that he had wrecked the Versailles settlement. The British tacitly confirmed this in June when they signed a treaty permitting Germany to build a navy one-third the size of Britain's. Germany was again one of the great powers, and Hitler began to formulate his plans for European domination.

Hitler's dramatic display of diplomatic strength irritated his fellow dictator, Benito Mussolini. Coming to power eleven years before Hitler, Mussolini regarded himself as the model fascist statesman, and he was eager to score triumphs of his own in foreign policy. His major objective was to carve out a great empire in East Africa, where Italy had a foothold in Somaliland and Eritrea on the border of the independent kingdom of Ethiopia. In 1896 the Italians had suffered a disastrous defeat by the Ethiopians at Adowa, and Mussolini anticipated the glory and revenge of an Italian conquest of Ethiopia. After thirteen years of posturing and strutting, he intended to make good his boasts of Italy's stature as a world power.

On December 5, 1934, Italian and Ethiopian troops clashed at Walwal, a desert oasis sixty miles inside Ethiopia which had been occupied by Italian forces for several years. The Italian troops were able to maintain possession of the outpost, killing over a hundred Ethiopians. Mussolini had been seeking such an incident for years, and he immediately demanded an apology and the payment of an indemnity of $100,000. Emperor Haile Selassie of Ethiopia, a proud and stubborn man, refused to be intimidated. He turned to the League of Nations to deal with this new threat to world peace. The League Council avoided the issue by getting both parties to agree to arbitrate the Walwal incident, a procedure that merely postponed the ultimate showdown. While the arbitration dragged on, Mussolini sent a steady stream of troops into his African colonies to prepare for war. In August 1935 Britain and France, fearful that war in Africa would give Hitler a free hand in Europe, tried to reach a settlement with Italy outside the League. Mussolini spurned all efforts at compromise, and finally in September Sir Samuel Hoare, the new British Foreign Secretary, made a dramatic announcement at Geneva. "The League stands," Hoare declared, "and my country stands with it for the collective maintenance of the Covenant in its entirety, and particularly for steady, collective resistance to all acts of unprovoked aggression."[1] Two days later Premier Pierre Laval of France pledged his support for the British position. Europe now faced its gravest crisis since the assassination of Archduke Ferdinand at Sarajevo in 1914.

The ominous developments in Europe gradually shattered the shell of American apathy. German rearmament and the threat of Italian aggression gave a sudden reality to the abstract issues of foreign policy, awakening the American people to dangers far more perilous than depression and unemployment. Virtually all Americans agreed that the nation must avoid involvement in the imminent war, but how best to

[1]Whitney H. Shepardson, *The United States in World Affairs, 1934–1935* (New York, 1935), p. 250.

achieve this clear-cut national objective was bitterly debated. For the next five years isolationists and internationalists sought to convince the majority of their countrymen of the wisdom of their policies, with the ultimate verdict resting on the course of events abroad.

The crux of the debate was the inevitability of war. The advocates of collective security argued that war could be prevented if the United States abandoned its aloof policy and stood behind the League of Nations and the Western democracies. Their most eloquent spokesman was Henry L. Stimson, the former Secretary of State who had embraced collective security during the Manchurian crisis. Returning to his law practice when the Democrats came into office in 1933, Stimson nevertheless continued to influence American policy. Cordell Hull privately sought Stimson's advice on a number of occasions, and Stimson spoke out publicly in speeches and letters to the editor of the New York *Times*. His basic theme never altered. The Kellogg-Briand Pact had made aggressive war a crime, and all peace-loving nations were obligated to join an international "sheriff's posse" to curb the disturbers of world peace. Stimson saw collective action as a moral and legal duty, but he was further convinced that it provided the only certain way to prevent another world war. Addressing the American Society of International Law in April 1935, Stimson summed up the internationalist credo when he declared, "The only certain way to keep out of a great war is to prevent that war from taking place, and the only hope of preventing war or even successfully restricting it is by the earnest, intelligent and unselfish cooperation of the nations of the world towards that end."[2]

Isolationists rejected the collective security formula. They believed that Europe was destined for an endless round of wars until the Continent was completely ravaged. The only wise course was to avoid the contagion by severing all ties with the European political system. John Bassett Moore, the most distinguished authority on international law in the country, affirmed the fundamentals of the isolationist position in an

[2]*Proceedings of the American Society of International Law, 1935* (Washington, 1935), p. 129.

article in *Foreign Affairs* in 1933. Moore insisted that war was inevitable, and that it was the duty of the United States to safeguard its own best interests by maintaining a strict neutrality. "The struggle for existence still continues and it will go on," Moore asserted. "As one long and intimately acquainted with men of arms, I may say that they do not share the new view that peace and tranquillity on earth may be promoted and stabilized by boycotts . . . and by the extension of the area of wars."[3]

Surprisingly, it was the internationalist Charles Warren who provided the isolationists with a detailed blueprint for ironclad American abstention from European war. As Assistant Attorney General during the First World War, Warren had experienced first hand the difficulty in maintaining neutral rights in wartime. At a symposium of the Council on Foreign Relations in January 1934, Warren proposed that the United States surrender many of its traditional neutral rights in order to avoid involvement in future world wars. His plan, which appeared in the April issue of *Foreign Affairs*, called for legislation to forbid the export of arms to belligerents, to ban loans by private bankers to governments at war, and to prevent American citizens from traveling on belligerent ships. Warren asserted that the last war proved that these rights were totally disregarded by the warring nations, and that the attempted defense of them led to American participation in the conflict. Although Warren felt that the nation could best protect itself by cooperating with other nations to prevent war, he endorsed his proposals as the next best way to avoid American involvement. "It is better that our citizens should run the risk of commercial loss," Warren asserted, "than that the country should be involved in a war to protect their alleged commercial rights."[4]

Warren's article had an immediate impact on American foreign policy. Secretary of State Hull asked a State Department committee to begin a careful analysis of the proposals,

[3]John Bassett Moore, "An Appeal to Reason," *Foreign Affairs*, XI (July 1933), 587.

[4]Charles Warren, "Troubles of a Neutral," *Foreign Affairs*, XII (April 1934), 391.

and this committee finally asked Warren to prepare a memorandum on his program. In August Warren submitted a 210-page document which contained recommendations and arguments for the self-denying measures he had suggested in his article — an arms embargo, a ban on loans, and a prohibition on travel on belligerent ships. The State Department forwarded this report to President Roosevelt, and he ordered the department to prepare draft legislation to carry out Warren's ideas. When a draft bill was framed in early 1935, a split developed inside the department over the arms embargo feature. Hull's legal advisers told him that the embargo would have to apply impartially to all belligerents according to international law. Norman Davis protested vigorously that such a policy would prevent the United States from cooperating with other nations to halt aggression. Davis proposed that the administration return to its 1933 position and insist that the President be given the power to embargo arms to aggressors. Davis had raised the central issue. In recasting its neutrality policy, the United States would have to choose between efforts to avert the outbreak of a major war or attempts to stay clear of inevitable conflict.

II

While the State Department wrestled with the complex problem of neutrality, the Nye committee continued its probe of the munitions industry. In their zeal to expose the merchants of death, the committee members had embarrassed several foreign governments with indiscreet disclosures, and Hull had asked President Roosevelt to meet with the Senators in order to restrain their activities. On March 19, 1935, the committee members came to the White House. Roosevelt suddenly injected a new issue in the meeting. Stating that he had always believed Secretary of State Bryan right in demanding that Americans not travel on belligerent ships, the President urged the committee to study the whole issue of neutrality and prepare appropriate legislation. The astonished Senators, who had not planned to make any legislative proposals on neutrality, now felt that they had a mandate from the President.

On April 9 Senator Nye joined with Senator Bennett C. Clark of Missouri, the ranking Democrat on the committee, to introduce two neutrality resolutions in Congress. The first authorized the President to withhold passports from American citizens traveling in war zones; the second forbade loans by private citizens to foreign governments at war. A month later Nye and Clark introduced a third resolution—an impartial embargo on the shipment of arms to all belligerents. This threefold neutrality program thus embodied the isolationist response to the growing danger of war in Europe. The United States would prepare for the conflict by adopting automatic devices to safeguard the nation from all risk of involvement.

The Nye-Clark measures won a mixed response. The peace societies rallied to their support, holding "Keep America Out of War" rallies, bombarding Congressmen with telegrams and letters, and sponsoring weekly radio broadcasts pleading for rigid neutrality. Internationalists were bitterly critical. The *Nation* ridiculed the idea of attempting to hide from a major world conflict. A speaker at a dinner session of the Foreign Policy Association called the resolutions cowardly, and warned that "you can't turn the American eagle into a turtle."[5]

Secretary of State Hull was disillusioned. He had not expected President Roosevelt to direct the Nye Committee toward neutrality legislation, and he now tried to undo the damage. Senator Key Pittman promised to bottle up the resolutions in his Foreign Relations Committee. But on July 26, to Hull's amazement, the Senate committee reported out the loan and travel resolutions. The Secretary sent Norman Davis to confer with Pittman, and after several unhappy exchanges they finally reached a compromise. When Hull appeared before the Foreign Relations Committee on July 10, the Senators agreed to recall the two resolutions and hold up action on the arms embargo proposal in return for Hull's promise that the State Department would cooperate with the committee in framing a comprehensive neutrality measure.

Hull had hoped to kill the neutrality program—he had only won a delay. Senator Nye, determined to see his resolutions

[5]New York *Times*, April 23, 1935, p. 5.

adopted at the current session of Congress, planned a filibuster with George Norris and Robert La Follette. Meanwhile,
the State Department prepared to meet with a subcommittee
of the Senate Foreign Relations Committee to hammer out a
neutrality proposal. Davis finally won the department over to
his concept of a discriminatory arms embargo, and President
Roosevelt concurred in late July. But when the State Department delegation conferred with the Senators, a deadlock soon
developed. With increasingly serious reports on the Ethiopian
crisis, the mood of Congress became strongly isolationist. Nye
continued his plans for a filibuster, convinced that he could
command enough votes to pass his program once he pried it
loose from the committee.

On August 19 the Senate Foreign Relations Committee met
to consider neutrality legislation. After an administration
move to postpone all such proposals to the next session was
defeated, the committee agreed to report out a bill containing
a mandatory arms embargo and a ban on travel on belligerent
ships. The Senators then adjourned so that Pittman could
draft the legislation. A few hours later Stephen Early,
Roosevelt's press secretary, telephoned Pittman that the President had just signed a letter prepared by the State Department
requesting Pittman to sponsor a discriminatory arms embargo
resolution. The Nevada Senator exploded. He told Early that
Roosevelt was "riding for a fall if he insists . . . on designating
the aggressor in accordance with the wishes of the League of
Nations." Pittman finally agreed to introduce such a measure
without comment, but as he told Early, Roosevelt "will be
licked sure as hell."[6] When Early reported this conversation to
the President, Roosevelt decided to withdraw the letter to Pittman and give up the fight for a discriminatory embargo.

At three o'clock on the afternoon of August 20 Senator Nye
and his associates, unaware of Roosevelt's surrender, began
their filibuster in the Senate. Threatening to keep Congress in
session until winter if necessary, speaker after speaker warned

[6]Memorandum of a telephone conversation between Stephen Early and
Key Pittman, August 19, 1935, President's Personal File 745, Franklin D.
Roosevelt Papers, Roosevelt Library, Hyde Park, N.Y.

of the imminent war in Europe and the need to redefine American neutral rights. As the filibuster continued, members of the Senate Foreign Relations Committee went out to find the hard-drinking Pittman and sober him up. At six o'clock Pittman entered the Senate chamber to introduce the bill containing the impartial arms embargo. Senator Nye and his cohorts jubilantly ended the debate, and the Senators adjourned after agreeing to act on the bill the next day. So ended one of the shortest and most successful filibusters in the history of the Senate.

At noon the next day Senator Pittman received permission to take up the neutrality bill out of order, and after the briefest of debates the measure passed without a dissenting vote. Many of the Senators had not even read the bill; one told a State Department aide that all he knew was that he had just voted to keep the United States out of war! Those who did read the bill discovered that it required the President to levy an impartial arms embargo "upon the outbreak or during the progress of war between, or among, two or more foreign states," authorized the President at his discretion to proclaim that American citizens traveling on belligerent ships did so at their own risk, and created a National Munitions Control Board to license and supervise the export of arms from the United States. The arms embargo feature was the vital part of the legislation. It meant that in case of a major war the United States would be compelled to deny the shipment of arms to all belligerents, regardless of American sympathies and interests. The embargo was limited to arms, ammunition, and implements of war as defined by the President, and did not include food, raw materials, or other categories of manufactured goods which would be as important to a belligerent as weapons in long conflicts.

The Senate action disturbed State Department officials. After a three-hour conference with his aides Secretary Hull decided to urge the President to have the bill killed in the House of Representatives. Roosevelt's own feelings about the measure wavered. In the morning he told a delegation of isolationist Congressmen that he was completely opposed to the Pittman bill. Yet that evening, when Hull conferred with him at the White House, the President rejected his advice to bury the legislation in the House. Instead, Roosevelt jotted down a memorandum for the House leaders, suggesting some technical changes in the measure and limiting it to a six-month period. The House approved the bill with Roosevelt's revisions, and the Senate accepted the changes on August 24. Roosevelt ended all speculation of a possible veto when he announced at his press conference on August 28 that the neutrality bill was "entirely satisfactory" to him. The next day Hull sent him a memorandum containing a draft statement criticizing the impartial arms embargo for Roosevelt to issue when he signed the legislation. To Hull's amazement, the President not only used this statement but added some stronger language to it. Thus when he signed the neutrality act on August 31, 1935, Roosevelt warned that the impartial arms embargo "might have exactly the opposite effect from that which was intended. In other words, the inflexible provisions might drag us into war instead of keeping us out."[7]

Although Hull and many internationalists felt that the President had followed a very cautious and compromising policy on neutrality legislation, Roosevelt was more consistent than his critics realized. From the outset he had felt the need for a more rigorous neutrality policy to prevent the United States from being dragged into a European war on legalistic grounds. He had approved the Warren memorandum and had led the Nye committee into this area in order to secure legislation which would free him from Wilson's dilemma in 1915. If war came in Europe, Roosevelt did not want to be forced to defend American commercial interest blindly—he would prefer to conduct American policy free from emotional and economic pressures and with sole regard to fundamental national interests. Most of all, he wanted flexible legislation allowing him a large degree of executive leadership. In this sense, the mandatory arms embargo disappointed him. But, always the pragmatist, he realized that if war broke out between Italy and Ethiopia, the impartial arms embargo would

---

[7]Department of State, *Peace and War: United States Foreign Policy, 1931–1941* (Washington, 1943), p. 272.

operate against Italy, which had the shipping and the financial resources to purchase arms from the United States—not
against Ethiopia which had neither. Thus Roosevelt suggested
the six-month limit. The temporary law would work favorably
in the short run, and when it expired he could prevail on Congress to give him the discretionary authority he really wanted.
To Roosevelt, who had just pushed a revolutionary series of
reforms through Congress in "the Second Hundred Days," the
1935 Neutrality Act seemed to be a reasonable compromise.
Five years later he expressed regret over signing the bill, and
historians, viewing his action with even longer perspective,
criticized him bitterly. But given the intensely isolationist
mood of the nation in 1935 and the great fear of war, his action is understandable.

III

The Neutrality Act of 1935 met its first test only five weeks
after passage by Congress. At dawn on October 3, 1935, the
Italian army invaded Ethiopia without a formal declaration of
war. The State Department relayed the news of the hostilities
to the President, who was cruising in the Pacific off the coast
of Baja California. A series of urgent telegraphic exchanges
took place, and on October 5 the State Department issued
proclamations recognizing a state of war between Italy and
Ethiopia, embargoing the export of arms to both countries,
and warning Americans not to travel on ships of either
belligerent. In addition, Hull released a statement by the
President warning Americans who engaged in trade with
either belligerent that they did so at their own risk.

The Roosevelt administration had embarked on a bold neutrality policy. The travel warning was, as Hull told Roosevelt,
"a gratuitous affront" to Italy since landlocked Ethiopia posed
no danger to Americans sailing on Italian ships. In recognizing a state of war, the administration was ignoring the advice
of its European diplomatic representatives and acting in advance of the League of Nations. Roosevelt, hoping to en-
courage the members of the League without opening himself

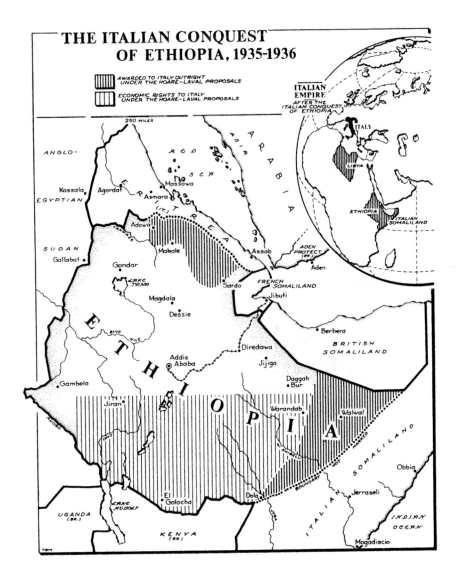

THE ITALIAN CONQUEST
OF ETHIOPIA, 1935-1936

to the charge of following in their footsteps, had persuaded a reluctant Hull to anticipate the world body. The trade warning had the same objective. If the League adopted sanctions against Italy, Roosevelt wanted to discourage, in so far as he could, American trade with the aggressor. The President displayed a high degree of ingenuity in using an isolationist Neutrality Act to fulfill collective security goals.

Two days later the Council of the League of Nations met at Geneva and formally condemned the Italian invasion of Ethiopia as a violation of the Covenant. For the first time since the founding of the League, the Council took steps to apply economic sanctions against a member. On October 10 a Co-ordination Committee met to consider what form the sanctions would take. On the same day Hull again urged American businessmen to avoid trade in war materials with the belligerents. Hull denied that this "moral embargo," as he later called it, was directed against Italy; the sole objective was "keeping this country out of war." When League officials approached the State Department about joining in possible sanctions, Hull piously answered that the United States would follow "an independent and affirmative policy."[8] The Co-ordination Committee then voted to ask League members to embargo the export of a long list of raw materials to Italy beginning on November 18. Oil, the most crucial of all Italian imports, was missing from the list on the grounds that non-League members could supply it. France and Britain refused to embargo oil fearing that Italy would declare war in retaliation. Thus the League decided to adopt sanctions strong enough to antagonize Italy but too weak to halt Mussolini's African adventure.

While the League powers equivocated on the sanctions issue, the Roosevelt administration struggled to insure American cooperation. On October 30 Roosevelt and Hull issued public statements again calling on the business community to avoid excessive trade with Italy and Ethiopia. Nevertheless, American exports, particularly of petroleum, began to rise sharply. In mid-November, three days before the League's

[8] *Ibid*, pp. 283-84.

modest sanctions were due to take effect, Hull disclosed that there had been significant increases in the sale of oil, copper, and scrap iron to Italy, and he hinted that the government might publish the names of those firms engaging in this trade. This threat helped to limit American commerce with Italy, much to the disgust of the exporters and the Italian-American community, who protested furiously. The administration held firm, and in the last three months of the year exports to Italy increased less than 20% over the 1934 average.

Collective security was not sabotaged by the United States; it was the leading powers of the League — Britain and France — who undermined the united stand against Mussolini. On December 10, French journalists revealed the details of a plan prepared by Sir Samuel Hoare and Pierre Laval, the erstwhile champions of the Covenant, to end the war in Africa by selling out Ethiopia. The Hoare-Laval plan proposed an "adjustment" of territory which would give Italy 60,000 acres of Ethiopian land in return for a grant of 3000, as well as award Italy exclusive economic rights for half of Ethiopia. The premature publication of the plan raised a great outcry in Britain. Hoare was forced to resign as Foreign Secretary, to be replaced by Anthony Eden, and the British government repudiated the scheme. But the damage had been done. The League continued to apply minor sanctions, but none on oil. Mussolini's forces pressed on, and aided by planes, tanks, and even poison gas, they quickly overwhelmed Haile Selassie's mountain tribesmen. In early May of 1936 Addis Ababa fell, the Emperor fled into exile, and Mussolini completed the conquest of Ethiopia.

The failure of the League in the Ethiopian crisis could not have been more complete. Faced with flagrant aggression, the League powers had half-heartedly invoked economic sanctions and then had lost their nerve. Collective security, the Wilsonian formula for world peace, proved unworkable. No great power was willing to risk war to preserve peace. "Fifty-two nations had combined to resist aggression"; A. J. P. Taylor has written, "all they accomplished was that Haile Selassie lost all his country instead of only half."[9] Apologists for the League

[9] *The Origins of the Second World War* (London, 1961), p. 95.

blamed the absence of the United States from the world body for the failure, but this was more rationalization than valid explanation. The United States pursued a bold and reasonably effective policy of cooperation with the League. Roosevelt and Hull took serious political risks, alienating the normally Democratic Italian-American community, to prevent American business from destroying the League blockade. When England and France ignored these overtures and chose appeasement, American foreign policy returned to its isolationist mold. A rare opportunity to realign the United States behind the League and the existing balance of power had been lost.

IV

The vital issues raised by the Ethiopian crisis determined the course of the debate on extending neutrality legislation when Congress reconvened in January 1936. With the 1935 act due to expire on February 29, the State Department framed a comprehensive measure for the Congressional committees to consider. Accepting the impartial arms embargo as inevitable, the administration proposal stressed the need to regulate trade in raw materials and manufactured items other than weapons by authorizing the President to limit trade in these goods with belligerents to a quota based on normal prewar levels. In addition, the legislation drafted by the State Department included the ban on loans to governments at war which Nye and Clark had wanted the year before. By offering concessions to the isolationists on the arms embargo and the loan ban, the administration clearly hoped to gain discretionary powers for the President on trade in strategic materials. Then if a war broke out in which the aggressor controlled the sea, Roosevelt could place severe restraints on American trade, while if the victim of aggression happened to have access to American markets, the President could permit supplies to flow without interruption. Thus the crux of the legislative fight would be the granting of presidential discretion.

In January the Senate and House committees began hearings on the State Department bill which revealed the complexity and confusion of the neutrality issue. From all quarters attacks were made on the administration's proposal. Advocates of mandatory neutrality were critical of the discretionary features, charging that the President would have the power to align the United States against aggressors and thus lead the nation into war. These witnesses urged that the trade quotas be made inflexible, and some even wanted to ban all trade with belligerents. "I would just as soon close every port in the United States, including Houston and Galveston," declared Representative Maury Maverick of San Antonio, "if it would save the life of one human being."[10] Another group of isolationists, led by Senator Borah, protested on grounds of nationalism against any restraints on American trade beyond the embargo on arms. Raising high the banner of international law, these Senators, who represented cotton, oil, and copper states which would suffer most from quotas on raw materials, demanded that Americans continue to enjoy complete freedom of the seas. They were seconded in their arguments by Italian-Americans, who claimed that the administration wanted the power to place quotas on trade with Italy in order to support League sanctions. Requesting a neutrality policy favoring Italy, one prominent citizen of Italian descent declared that it would be "positively un-American" to grant the President discretionary powers.

This discordant chorus of objections proved to be too powerful for the administration. On February 7, when Congressional leaders reported that there was no chance of passage for the State Department measure, Roosevelt responded by agreeing to accept an extension of the existing act for another year. After very brief debates in both Houses, Congress passed a bill continuing the 1935 Neutrality Act until May 1, 1937, with the addition of the ban on loans to belligerent governments. Roosevelt signed the bill on February 29 without comment. The same day he issued a statement calling on American businessmen to continue to limit their trade with Italy and Ethiopia. This appeal was a poor substitute for the powers that Congress had denied him.

[10]"American Neutrality Policy," *Hearings* before the House Committee on Foreign Affairs, 74th Cong., 2nd Sess. (Washington, 1936), p. 99.

On March 7, one week after President Roosevelt signed the 1936 Neutrality Act, Adolf Hitler informed ambassadors of Belgium, France, Great Britain, and Italy that Germany considered the Locarno Treaty dead. Hitler then went directly to the Reichstag, told the legislators of the drastic step he had taken, and boldly announced that at that very moment German troops were marching into the Rhineland in defiance of the Treaty of Versailles. Thus in a matter of hours the German dictator had challenged the two treaties designed to prevent Germany from regaining hegemony in Europe. The military reoccupation of the Rhineland, that part of Germany west of the Rhine bordering on France and Belgium, threatened French security by exposing France to potential assault by German forces moving through Belgium as they had in 1915, and thus bypassing the Maginot Line along the common Franco-German frontier. Hitler was taking the first of his great gambles, betting that the tensions created by the Ethiopian crisis would inhibit any retaliatory action by France and Britain. The risks were enormous, for the new German army was still in the process of formation, but Hitler believed that the psychological weaknesses of his opponents would more than offset their enormous military superiority.

Hitler was right. Within three days his soldiers had occupied the entire Rhineland while British and French statesmen floundered. The victors of World War I were unwilling to risk a war to stop Hitler in 1936, even a war which they were certain of winning. They decided to pass the responsibility for maintaining peace to the League of Nations, which was on the verge of dissolution as a result of the failure in Ethiopia. When the League Council met in London on March 14, the members quickly passed a resolution condemning Germany for violating the treaties of Versailles and Locarno. But instead of recommending sanctions for this act of international lawlessness, as the Soviet representative advocated, the Council invited Hitler to propose a new security system for Europe. Hitler obliged, stating that he had no territorial claims in Europe and suggesting a twenty-five year nonaggression pact. Efforts to elucidate his ambiguous proposals proved fruitless, and the Rhineland affair gradually subsided. Hitler had taken a major step toward German primacy in Europe.

In the United States this recent German feat tended to reinforce the prevailing isolationist climate. Secretary viewed the episode as a European development which did affect the United States. When the French asked the America government to condemn the German action on moral grounds, Hull rejected the plea and even refused to allow any American diplomatic representatives to attend the Council meetings of the League in London. At the Democratic national convention in June the adminstration's response to the deepening European crisis was sharpened. The party platform plank on foreign affairs was a paraphrase of Senator Nye's ideas. "We shall continue to observe a true neutrality in the disputes of others;" the platform stated, "to work for peace and to take the profits out of war; to guard against being drawn, by political commitments, international banking, or private trading, into any war which may develop anywhere."[11] Those who believed that the President himself did not share these sentiments were rudely shaken by Roosevelt's only major campaign address on foreign affairs, at Chautauqua, New York, on August 14, 1936. "We are not isolationists except in so far as we seek to isolate ourselves completely from war. . . . I hate war. I have passed unnumbered hours, I shall pass unnumbered hours, thinking and planning how war may be kept from this nation." Echoing the "merchants of death" theme, Roosevelt went on to praise the new neutrality legislation Congress had given him and to assure the nation's voters that given the choice of profits or peace, he would unhesitatingly choose peace. Yet at the very end of his address, he moderated his militantly isolationist tone to remind his listeners that "international relations involve of necessity a vast uncharted area" in which the President and Secretary of State must have discretionary power to keep the nation at peace.[12]

By mid-1936 the general trend of international affairs was assuming an alarming pattern. The failure of the League in the Ethiopian crisis, the resurgence of German power made evident in the reoccupation of the Rhineland, and the ambivalence of Britain and France in meeting these challenges — all

[11]New York *Times*, June 26, 1936, p. 13.
[12]*Peace and War*, pp. 326-28.

indicated the breakdown of the Versailles system and the imminence of war. Viewing the events of 1936, the author of the
Council on Foreign Relations' annual survey of American foreign policy wrote that throughout the year the American people "came to fear that another general war was in the making,
more destructive than the last, and that its Day was not far off.
Such a catastrophe may occur in 1937, in 1940, or never."[13]
This realistic appraisal, shared by informed people inside and
outside the government, intensified the American desire to
sever all ties with a Europe about to go up in flames. At the
time, and ever since, internationalists charged that it was precisely this American refusal to play a responsible role in maintaining a stable Europe that made war inevitable. This simple
view fails to do justice to the dilemma facing the United States.
Given the unwillingness, indeed the inability, of Britain and
France to stand behind their own vital interests in Europe, and
the total failure of the League of Nations, it would have been a
remarkable act of faith for the United States to embrace collective security. A strong stand by the Western democracies
might have permitted Roosevelt to offer American support,
but British and French appeasement compelled the United
States to seek security by insulating itself from Europe. The
European appeasers were in a very real sense the co-authors of
American neutrality policy.

V

The armed prelude to the Second World War in Europe began on July 18, 1936; in colonial Morocco a group of Spanish
generals revolted against the Republican government. The
uprising by the army was immediately successful. But when
army garrisons in Spain rebelled, they were besieged by angry
crowds who rallied to support the government. The failure of
the navy to join the uprising endangered the plan to ferry the
army units from Morocco over to Spain until General Francis-

[13]Whitney H. Shepardson, *The United States in World Affairs, 1936*
(New York, 1937), p. 1.

co Franco, who had become the leader of the Rebels, arranged for an airlift by thirty German Junker transports. From this point on, Germany and Italy gave increasing aid to the Spanish rebels in their effort to overthrow the Republican regime. The intervention of the Fascist powers in what had begun as a civil war led the Soviet Union to send arms, volunteers, and supplies to the Loyalists (Republicans). Britain and France, fearful that the fighting in Spain would spread into a general European conflict, took the lead in creating a Non-Intervention Committee which included Germany, Italy, the Soviet Union, and twenty other European states. With headquarters in London, this committee tried to prevent the shipment of arms to either side in Spain. Since Germany, Italy, and the Soviet Union continued to supply their favorites, the major contribution of the committee was to deny the Spanish Republicans, the duly established and recognized government, the traditional right to purchase goods from such member countries as Britain and France. Under the banner of nonintervention, the Western democracies were abetting the cause of Fascism in Spain.

The Spanish Civil War had a profound impact on the United States. While the majority of the people viewed it somewhat passively, fearful only that it might lead to a general European war, American Catholics and left-wing political groups responded passionately to the fighting in Spain. For Catholics it was a holy war in which Communist-inspired atheists were attempting to destroy the Church. For them Franco was not a dictator but a Spanish George Washington, fighting to free his country of Communism and establish religious and political order. The American left-wing, ranging from the main body of New Deal liberals through the more militant radicals and socialists to the Communist party members and fellow travelers, saw the war as a death struggle between democracy, embodied in the Republican cause, and Fascism, represented by the Rebels. The Spanish Civil War mobilized interest in foreign affairs among liberals who had been immersed in domestic problems since the onset of the depression. College professors, Protestant ministers, writers, actors and actresses, social workers, union leaders, journalists, college students — intellectuals and pseudo-intellectuals found in the Spanish Loyalists a cause which evoked total commitment and dedication. Committees were formed and reformed; mass meetings adopted resolution after resolution; the pages of liberal journals bulged with angry letters; brigades of young men sailed for Spain, many to give their lives for their beliefs. More than any other event of the 1930s, the Spanish Civil War vividly aroused the American people to the compelling pattern of European affairs. It was not merely a tragedy to be mourned from afar; it was an experience that touched the lives and the hearts of millions of Americans.

The Spanish Civil War raised a series of difficult policy decisions for the Roosevelt adminstration. Secretary of State Hull approved the formation of the Non-Intervention Committee in Europe, but was greatly relieved when Britain and France did not ask the United States to join. He wanted to cooperate with the Western democracies, but he dared not arouse an isolationist clamor by doing so openly. On August 7, 1936, Hull notified American diplomatic and consular agents in Spain that while the arms embargo did not apply to a civil war, the government hoped that American citizens would "scrupulously refrain from any interference whatsoever in the unfortunate Spanish situation."[14] Four days later the State Department released the Secretary's statement to the public. Later in the month the department announced that the Glenn L. Martin Company had asked whether the government would object to the sale of eight bombers to the Spanish Republicans. In a reply made public on August 22, Acting Secretary of State William Phillips told the Martin Company that such a sale would violate the spirit of American foreign policy. Thus by the end of the first month of the Spanish Civil War, the United States had adopted a moral embargo against the sale of war materials to either side in Spain.

Surprisingly, the administration's policy met with approval. Isolationists praised Hull for stern action to prevent American involvement in a European war; internationalists applauded

[14]*Foreign Relations of the United States: 1936* (5 volumes, Washington, 1953-1954), II, 471.

him for cooperating so closely with Britain and France. But those who sympathized with the Loyalists objected strongly, pointing out that the refusal to sanction trade with an established government was a complete reversal of traditional American practice in civil wars. Despite these objections American exporters observed the State Department's moral embargo through the fall of 1936. Then in December Robert Cuse, a New Jersey scrap dealer, defied the government by signing a contract to export nearly $3 million worth of airplane parts and engines to the Spanish government. The Department was compelled to issue the export licenses, though at a press conference on December 28 Roosevelt condemned Cuse as unpatriotic.

Cuse's breach of the moral embargo led the administration to seek special legislation to extend the arms embargo to the Spanish Civil War. When Congress convened on January 6, administration spokesmen introduced identical Spanish arms embargo resolutions in both Houses and asked for immediate action so that the government could stop the Cuse shipment, which was being loaded on the Spanish freighter *Mar Cantábrico* in New York harbor. After very brief debate both chambers approved the embargo on January 7, with the sole dissenting vote coming from Representative John Toussaint Bernard, a Farmer-Laborite from Minnesota, who charged that the resolution would aid Fascists "in the open rape of Spain."[15] Despite the unprecedented speed with which Congress acted, technicalities prevented the embargo from going into effect until the next day. Meanwhile, the *Mar Cantábrico* had sailed from New York, followed to the territorial limit by Coast Guard cutters and patrol planes waiting for last minute orders to stop her voyage. Robert Cuse won only a temporary reprieve. Spanish Rebels intercepted the *Mar Cantábrico* as it approached Spain, and the airplanes and engines eventually contributed to Franco's deadly air attacks on the Republicans.

As the Spanish Civil War continued and the Rebels gained the upper hand, the embargo became increasingly unpopular in the United States. Many advocates of strict neutrality, led

[15]*Congressional Record*, January 21, 1937, Appendix, p. 65.

by Senator Nye, eventually urged its removal, but the administration remained adamant and the embargo continued until the final victory of Franco's forces in the spring of 1939. At the time many critics charged that the administration retained the embargo on Spain out of fear of antagonizing American Catholics. Undoubtedly this was an important factor in the policy decision, but it was not the decisive one. More important was the determination of Hull and Roosevelt to cooperate with Britain and France in trying to contain the Civil War in Spain. Roosevelt's own sympathies were with the Loyalists, but Hull helped persuade him that the danger of a general war made it imperative to halt the flow of American supplies to Spain. Thus the United States, which refused throughout the 1930s to cooperate with other nations for collective security, was willing to collaborate in appeasement.

VI

The passage of the Spanish arms embargo was the prelude to full scale Congressional action on neutrality legislation in 1937. The original act, extended in 1936, was due to expire on May 1, 1937. Congress had only four months to arrive at a final decision on the complex issues it had dodged in the last session. The basic goal, keeping the nation out of any major European war that might occur, had not changed, but there were still a bewildering variety of solutions being advocated inside and outside of Congress. The basic features of neutrality adopted in 1935 and 1936—the impartial arms embargo, the ban on travel, the prohibition of loans to belligerent governments—were not in question. The debatable issue was to what extent the nation was willing to sacrifice its export trade in goods other than arms if war came in Europe. By early 1937 the United States was slowly climbing out of the depression and was looking forward to complete economic recovery. The task confronting Congress was to frame a neutrality act that would insure peace without endangering prosperity.

It was Bernard M. Baruch, the financier and confidant of presidents, who came up with the cash-and-carry formula to keep the United States neutral without sacrificing the profits of foreign trade. In magazine articles in 1935 and 1936 Baruch argued that it was the shipment of goods to belligerents, not the sale, that involved the risk for the nation. Therefore, he suggested the cash-and-carry principle — "We will sell to any belligerent anything except lethal weapons, but the terms are *'cash on the barrel-head and come and get it.'* "[16] Baruch's ingenious plan was designed to avoid repetition of the incidents that had led to war in 1917. When American goods were sold to a belligerent, title to the exports would pass immediately into the hands of the purchaser, who would not be permitted to transport them in American ships. By keeping American ships, goods, and citizens off the high seas in time of war, Baruch hoped to guarantee the continuation of American foreign trade without the risk of war. His formula was technically neutral, but it would always operate in favor of the belligerent with large cash reserves and control of the sea. But this limititation did not bother most Americans, who desired a policy where nothing was ventured and a great deal could be gained.

The cash-and-carry scheme won the favor of both the administration and the advocates of strict neutrality. Roosevelt liked the plan because it worked out in favor of England and France, the nations with sea power, and against Germany. When Senator Pittman introduced a comprehensive neutrality bill in January 1937, based on the cash-and-carry principle, the administration endorsed it and had a similar measure introduced in the House. Senator Nye had no objections to the Baruch plan. He preferred a total embargo on all trade with belligerents, but he realized that such a measure could not be passed and thus he was willing to accept cash-and-carry as a reasonable compromise. However, Nye and others who shared his views insisted that the Pittman bill contained too many provisions granting discretionary power to the President. They

[16]Bernard Baruch, "Neutrality," *Current History*, XLIV (June 1936), 43.

pressed for amendments to the administration measure which would compel the President to impose automatic restrictions on American trade in time of war. The conflict between discretionary and mandatory features dominated the debate in Congress.

In addition to the Nye group, there was a small band of men in Congress who found the cash-and-carry principle completely distasteful. Extreme nationalists like Senators Hiram Johnson and William Borah protested the surrender of traditional American neutral rights as cowardly and dishonorable. They insisted that the United States should stand firmly for freedom of the seas in time of war, and should not, as Johnson said, "sell goods and then hide." During the Senate debate, the two irreconcilable Senators referred to the cash-and-carry bill as a "British measure," claiming that it was designed not to preserve American neutrality but rather to assist Britain when war came. Calling upon the Senate to defeat the bill, Borah declared, "I believe in fighting for the substantial rights which are essential to the preservation of the economic welfare of the Nation."[17]

His colleagues did not agree. "I can't understand how anyone could weigh in the balance gold against blood," declared Senator Josh Lee, Democrat of Oklahoma.[18] When the vote was taken on the cash-and-carry bill in the Senate, it passed by an overwhelming margin, 63 to 6. A House Bill containing more discretion for the President was reported out of committee, and after surviving a motion for recommittal by a vote of 275 to 118, it won final approval with only thirteen dissenting votes. A grateful Congress had embraced Baruch's solution to the dilemma of choosing between peace and prosperity. By voting for cash-and-carry, the legislators chose both.

A number of discrepancies between House and Senate bills sent the neutrality legislation to a conference committee. For over a month Senator Pittman refused to surrender any of the more rigid features of his bill, but finally Presidential pressure broke the impasse. The conference committee adopted the

---

[17]*Congressional Record*, March 3, 1937, p. 1806.
[18]*Ibid*, p. 1796.

discretionary features of the House bill, and then both chambers gave their approval in late April. With the 1936 Neutrality Act due to expire in a few hours, a Navy seaplane flew the new legislation to President Roosevelt, who was relaxing on a fishing cruise far out in the Gulf of Mexico. At 6:30 A.M. on May 1 Roosevelt signed the new act.

The Neutrality Act of 1937 completed the two year search for a policy to keep the United States out of World War II. By its terms, whenever the President found a state of war to exist, he was compelled to place three major restrictions on the activities of American citizens—an embargo on arms, a ban on loans, and a prohibition on travel on belligerent ships. In theory, these limitations would prevent munitions makers, greedy bankers, and mad-cap travelers from plunging the nation into war as many believed they had in 1917. The 1937 act also gave the President discretionary authority to place all trade with belligerents under the cash-and-carry formula. Thus he could require American citizens to divest themselves of all title to exports sold to belligerents before the goods left the United States and he could bar the shipment of goods that he specified on American vessels traveling to belligerent countries. While the main part of the 1937 act was permanent, the discretionary cash-and-carry features were temporary, and would expire in May, 1939.

The Neutrality Act of 1937 was a compromise that reflected the contradictory desire of the American people to remain economically in the world and politically out of it. No single group in the nation was fully satisfied with the legislation. The advocates of rigid neutrality were pleased with the arms embargo, the loan ban, and the travel prohibition, but they disliked the discretionary cash-and-carry feature. They feared that these provisions would permit heavy trade with England and France in a general European war which would create the kind of economic ties that they believed were responsible for American entry into World War I. Borah and Johnson were also dismayed by the cash-and-carry provisions because they would sacrifice traditional American neutral rights on the high seas. Internationalists were equally unhappy, though for different reasons. They applauded the cash-and-carry plan, but remained bitterly critical of the impartial arms embargo which they felt played right into the hands of potential aggressors. Yet despite these mixed feelings, most Americans accepted the 1937 act as a major step toward keeping the United States out of the next war.

Foreign observers were outspoken in their evaluation of the neutrality legislation. In late March Neville Chamberlain, soon to be Prime Minister of England, wrote an American cabinet member that repeal of the arms embargo would be "the greatest single contribution which the United States could make at the present moment to the preservation of world peace."[19] But when the cash-and-carry plan was adopted in April, British and French diplomats realized how much it favored their countries and told William Bullitt, the American ambassador in Paris, that their governments were "extremely satisfied" with the 1937 act. Germany reacted adversely, seeing in cash-and-carry a pro-British policy; a Berlin newspaper stated that the legislation amounted virtually to an Anglo-American alliance. The Chinese were equally unhappy. Their potential enemy, Japan, with its powerful navy and control of the sea, would find cash-and-carry a great asset in any war with China.

These differing estimates reveal the inadequacy and haphazard character of neutrality legislation. As the world moved closer to a major war in the late 1930s, the United States adopted a highly equivocal policy which failed to promote basic national interests. Hypnotized by their own fear of war, the American people had chosen to support legslation which made war more likely by informing potential aggressors that the United States would abandon any effort to prevent the outbreak of hostilities and follow carefully delineated policies once they did occur. Instead of attempting to influence the course of international events, the United States had chosen, as one international lawyer expressed it, "a policy of scuttle and run to the storm cellar."[20] Only belatedly did the

[19]*Foreign Relations: 1937*, I, 100.
[20]*Proceedings of the American Society of International Law, 1937* (Washington, 1937), p. 179.

American people realize that they did have a stake in the European balance of power—that domination of the continent by an aggressive Germany would jeopardize the security of the United States. In a very real sense, the neutrality legislation misled Hitler, encouraging him to believe that America was indifferent to the fate of Europe.

CHAPTER III

A World at War

J UST BEFORE MIDNIGHT on July 7, 1937, a volley of shots rang out between Chinese and Japanese troops stationed near the Marco Polo bridge on the main railroad line connecting Peking and Central China. Thus the Pacific phase of World War II began only ten weeks after the passage of permanent neutrality legislation. Although a truce was arranged two days later, it lasted but a few hours. The fighting again stopped on July 11, but when Japan used this respite to rush reinforcements into China, any hope of heading off a major clash disappeared. By the end of the month heavy fighting was underway, which quickly led to the defeat of the Chinese forces and Japanese occupation of Peking. When the fighting spread to Shanghai in mid-August, the China Incident, as the Japanese referred to it, had become a full-scale war.

The Sino-Japanese war was the logical result of Japan's determination to dominate Asia. The seizure of Manchuria had marked the beginning, not the climax, of Japanese expansion in the Far East. Confronted with a population growing at the rate of one million a year and a basic scarcity of raw materials for an industrial economy, Japanese leaders were bent on exploiting the wealth of China. Civilian statesmen in Japan had planned traditional methods of trade and diplomacy to achieve this end, but in the 1930s the army leaders began to destroy the party system and take over the government. The militarists, fearful of both the expanding power of the Soviet Union in Siberia and the weak but ambitious Chinese government at Nanking under Chiang Kai-shek, were determined to dominate as much of China as possible. In 1935 and 1936 Japanese army leaders were undermining Chinese sovereignty in the five northern provinces bordering on Manchuria. They met with stubborn resistance from the Chinese Nationalists, who decided to challenge the Japanese to an all-out conflict rather than surrender their territory piecemeal.

The outbreak of war in the Far East came as a surprise to most Americans. Many observers had expressed concern in December, 1934, when the Japanese had announced their intention of withdrawing from the Five Power Treaty signed at the Washington Conference in 1922 to limit battleships and aircraft carriers. A year later at the London Naval Conference the United States and Great Britain rejected Japanese demands for naval equality. The Japanese responded by walking out of the conference and announcing a program of large-scale naval construction. Rebuffed by the Western democracies, Japan aligned herself with Germany in November, 1936, by signing an Anti-Comintern Pact. Although the open clauses of this treaty merely provided for cooperation between the two nations in resisting Communist propaganda and subversion, there were secret sections that virtually amounted to a defensive alliance against the Soviet Union.

Yet despite these signs of Japan's increasing restiveness, the United States was completely caught off-guard by the war in China. The initial response of the American government was very mild. Rejecting Chinese pleas for American mediation and British overtures for joint protests to Tokyo, Hull released a statement of moral principles on July 16, 1937, to which he asked other nations, including Japan, to subscribe. His answer came two weeks later when the Japanese army launched its offensive in North China. When the Japanese assault shifted to Shanghai, the major port of China and a center of American commercial interests, Hull announced that the government was dispatching 1200 marines to guard American lives and property in China. Clearly, while the United States would attempt to defend the interests of its citizens, it did not intend to uphold the Nine Power Treaty of 1922, to which Japan was a signatory, preserving the territorial integrity and political independence of China.

The immediate problem confronting the Roosevelt administration was whether or not to invoke the Neutrality Act in the Far Eastern war. Since no formal declaration of war had been issued by either side, the President could exercise discretion in regard to imposing the arms, travel, and loan bans, as well as the cash-and-carry provisions for general trade. The Neutrality Act would favor Japan, who produced her own munitions and who could put her control of the sea to maximum advantage if trade were placed on a cash-and-carry basis. China, on the other hand, needed to import arms from abroad and lacked both the ready cash and the ships to buy supplies on a come-and-get-it basis. After a long conference with his aides, Roosevelt announced at a press conference on August 7, 1937, that he was keeping the question of invoking the Neutrality Act on a "24-hour basis."[1] Despite a great outcry from isolationists in Congress, Roosevelt continued to withhold the Neutrality Act. On September 14, after the Japanese announcement of an extensive blockade of the Chinese coastline, the President did halt trade with China in government-owned ships and warned American exporters that they engaged in commerce with China at their own risk. This order had little effect on American shipping, which was largely privately owned, and the American people, sympathetic to China, generally approved of Roosevelt's refusal to invoke the Neutrality Act for the Far Eastern war.

In mid-September China appealed to the League of Nations. On October 6 the League Assembly found that Japan had violated the Nine Power Treaty and the Kellogg-Briand Pact and recommended that the signatories of the Nine Power Treaty call a conference to consider this violation. The Chinese were greatly encouraged, for only the day before President Roosevelt had delivered his Quarantine address in which he condemned "the epidemic of world lawlessness" then raging and called for "positive endeavors to preserve peace."[2] When Hull announced that the United States concurred in the

---

[1]Press Conference No. 392, August 17, 1937, Franklin D. Roosevelt Papers, PPF 1-P, X, 162.
[2]State Department, *Press Releases*, XVII (October 9, 1937), 276, 279.

JAPANESE AGGRESSION
IN CHINA, 1937

League judgment of Japan and would attend a conference at Brussels of all nations with interests in East Asia, it seemed as if American policy was undergoing a major reversal.

President Roosevelt dispelled any such thoughts in his Columbus Day address on October 12; the sole purpose of American policy at the Brussels conference would be to cooperate with China and Japan to seek an end to the fighting. The conference convened on November 3, and it quickly proved a fiasco. Neither Britain nor the United States was willing to take the lead against the Japanese, who refused even to attend the session. Only the Soviet Union recommended strong action, but Russian sincerity was never put to the test. When the conference adjourned on November 24, it had failed to take a single concrete step to aid China or restrain Japan. Indeed, the conference had probably thwarted the one real opportunity to end the fighting. In October, the Japanese leaders had made a set of moderate proposals to Chiang Kai-shek to halt the conflict. Chiang, believing that the United States and England were behind him, turned down the offers to await the outcome at Brussels. During the conference the military situation in China changed drastically—Japanese forces completed the conquest of Shanghai and routed the Chinese armies before Nanking. By early December Chiang was ready to negotiate with Japan, but the Japanese leaders now increased their demands until the Chinese preferred a losing war to submission.

The collective appeasement of the Brussels conference marked another step in the American retreat from the Open Door Policy. The United States had deep economic, religious, and emotional faith in the future of China, but when confronted with Japanese aggression, the American people preferred to withdraw from the Far East rather than risk war. When Japanese naval aviators bombed the American gunboat *Panay* on the Yangtze in December, there was a brief flurry of public indignation, but most people were relieved when Japan quickly apologized and paid an indemnity for this unprovoked attack. In 1938, following Japanese bombings of Chinese civilians, Secretary Hull inaugurated an unofficial but quite effective embargo on the export of aircraft to Japan. Americans, however, continued to supply Japan with very large quantities of petroleum and scrap iron which were essential to the Japanese war effort in China. Thus the United States tacitly assented to the Japanese sweep into China and gave Japan the dangerously misleading idea that the American government and people would acquiesce in future Japanese aggression in the Far East.

By the fall of 1937 the world was moving inexorably toward a second world war. The Japanese onslaught in China continued. When Nanking fell in December, the Chinese moved their capital to Chungking and announced that they intended to continue fighting in the rugged interior of China. In Spain the Rebels gradually gained the upper hand in the fighting. Aided by an Italian armored division and a German bombing squadron, Franco's forces revealed to a watching world the full horror of modern weapons of war. The Spanish Civil War also served to draw Hitler and Mussolini together as they cooperated in subverting the Non-Intervention Committee. In October 1936 the Rome-Berlin Axis came into being when Germany and Italy signed protocols settling differences between them. A year later Italy signed the Anti-Comintern Pact, thus creating the basis for a Rome-Berlin-Tokyo Axis. Three powerful and discontented powers had now joined together in a loose association while they continued their separate efforts to upset the existing balance of power.

The ambitions of Germany, Japan, and Italy posed serious threats to the long-range national interests of the United States. Although most Americans still wished to avoid war at all costs, President Roosevelt was beginning to assess the ultimate danger the nation faced from these three countries. His earlier proccupation with the domestic crisis passed as the nation slowly recovered from the depression and the New Deal reached completion. After the bitter court-packing fight, Roosevelt turned more and more to problems of foreign policy. Although he had not yet fully determined on specific policies to restore American initiative in world affairs, he now

began groping for ways to reverse the long drift into isolationism. In a letter to Colonel House in October 1937, the
President stated, "I verily believe that as time goes on we can
slowly but surely make people realize that war will be a greater
danger to us if we close all doors and windows than if we go out
in the street and use our influence to curb the riot."[3] Still
uncertain how far he wished to go and how far he could persuade the American people to go, Roosevelt began trying to
find his way out of the isolationist corner into which he had
backed in the early 1930s.

Roosevelt revealed his new interest in foreign affairs in the
Quarantine speech, delivered in Chicago on October 5, 1937.
In his first public address on foreign policy since the highly
isolationist Chautauqua speech fourteen months earlier, the
President spoke out boldly. "The peace, the freedom, and the
security of 90 percent of the population of the world is being
jeopardized by the remaining 10 percent, who are threatening
a breakdown of all international order and law." In a striking
figure of speech Roosevelt called for "a quarantine of the pa-
tients," which implied collective action against aggressors
without committing the United States to any specific line of
action. He kept his remaining remarks deliberately vague,
concluding, "America hates war, America hopes for peace.
Therefore, America actively engages in the search for peace."[4]

The Quarantine speech set off a predictable outcry in the
isolationist press, but the most notable result was the praise
which Roosevelt received in other quarters. The Washington
Post endorsed his remarks in a front-page editorial; the New
York *Times* gave him solid backing; even in the Middle West
the majority of editorials were sympathetic. No one seemed
more surprised by the unexpected approval than the President. At a press conference the next day, when reporters tried
to learn what positive peace efforts Roosevelt had in mind, the
President was evasive. Denying that his speech would be taken
as a repudiation of neutrality legislation, Roosevelt tried to

---

[3]Elliot Roosevelt, ed., *F.D.R.: His Personal Letters, 1928–1945* (2
vols.; New York, 1950), I, 719.
[4]State Department, *Press Releases*, XVII (October 9, 1937), 276–279.

convince the skeptical journalists that his remarks were entirely consistent with existing American policy. It seems doubtful that Roosevelt had any concrete scheme in mind, though he may have been thinking of some form of collective neutrality whereby the United States would band together with other neutrals to prevent the spread of war. He apparently had decided to test out American sentiment, expecting to find it overwhelmingly isolationist. When his speech met with vigorous approval, he retreated into ambiguity rather than confess that he was unprepared to give substance to his rhetoric.

But Roosevelt's speech did lead to one significant attempt to use American prestige and influence to alter the drift toward war. A few hours after Roosevelt's press conference on October 6, Under Secretary of State Sumner Welles met with him to offer a specific plan to follow up the Quarantine speech. Welles, a career diplomat and old friend of the President's, had been one of the chief architects of the administration's Good Neighbor policy in Latin America while serving as Assistant Secretary of State. In the spring of 1937 Roosevelt appointed him Under Secretary, much to the displeasure of Cordell Hull who resented Welles' close personal relationship with the President. In his new post Welles moved beyond the confines of Latin American affairs to deal with the worldwide problems confronting the nation. A staunch internationalist, he became convinced in the summer of 1937 that unless the United States assumed a new role of leadership in international affairs, the world would soon be engulfed in war.

At the October 6th conference with Roosevelt, Welles outlined a twofold scheme. First, he suggested that Roosevelt call the diplomatic representatives of all nations to the White House for the Armistice Day ceremonies on November 11. The President would then deliver an appeal to the assembled diplomats, and through them to all mankind, for a return to "those basic standards of international law which Western civilization had gradually and painfully evolved" as a first and indispensable step toward preserving world peace.[5] Welles

[5]Sumner Welles, *Seven Decisions That Shaped History* (New York, 1951), p. 17.

then wanted Roosevelt to pinpoint the arms race, economic barriers to trade, and neutral rights and obligations as the most pressing problems facing mankind, and ask the other nations if they would be willing to attend a world conference dealing with these topics. If the replies were favorable, the Welles plan called for the President to invite nine smaller nations to send delegates to Washington to draw up an agenda for the future world conference.

Roosevelt was delighted with the Welles plan because it offered him a way to continue his quest for peace without making any military or political commitments. Secretary of State Hull, however, found the plan completely unacceptable, telling the President that the scheme was likely to lull England and France into a false tranquility at a time when they had just begun the serious rearmament necessary to stand up to Hitler. Hull's principal objection to the proposal was undoubtedly personal, since what Welles had proposed was steeped in the vague moralizing that characterized the Secretary's approach to diplomacy. Nevertheless, Hull insisted that Britain and France should be sounded out before any move was made. Roosevelt, realizing that his Secretary of State was completely opposed to the Armistice Day appeal, quietly shelved the whole proposition.

In early January 1938 the administration reconsidered. Norman Davis, the American representative at the Brussels conference, strongly endorsed Welles' proposal and finally convinced Hull, who trusted him implicitly, to give the scheme a chance. Accordingly, in mid-January the State Department sent a note to Prime Minister Neville Chamberlain asking for his reaction to the idea of the United States taking preliminary steps toward calling an international conference along the lines Welles had suggested. The note arrived in London just when Chamberlain was embarking on a new attempt to reach an accommodation with Mussolini as part of his policy of appeasement toward the European dictators. Chamberlain, ignoring the advice of the British ambassador in Washington, sent back a cool reply stating that he was pursuing vital negotiations with Italy and requesting Roosevelt to postpone his overture. When Anthony Eden, the British Foreign Secretary, returned from a vacation in Southern France, he vigorously objected to Chamberlain's rebuff of the United States, and he finally persuaded the Prime Minister to send a more encouraging note in late January. But nothing short of a completely enthusiastic British reply would have offset Hull's continued skepticism, and Roosevelt once again abandoned the Welles scheme, this time permanently.

Winston Churchill has called the British rejection of the American plan for an international conference "the loss of the last frail chance to save the world from tyranny otherwise than by war," but it is difficult to see how Welles' proposal would have altered the course of events.[6] There was little chance that Germany, Italy, and Japan would agree with the United States, England, and France on meaningful standards of international conduct. The fundamental issues went far deeper than rearmament, trade barriers, and neutral rights—the topics Welles wanted discussed. Indeed, the plan is most interesting as an example of the naive American outlook on the world in 1937. This concern with legal and moral principles indicates the inability of American leaders to comprehend the threat posed by German, Italy, and Japan. The Axis nations were bent on upsetting the existing balance of power and imposing their own totalitarian order on the world. Nothing less than firm American military and political commitments was likely to deter them.

Although Franklin Roosevelt failed to reorient American foreign policy in the fall of 1937, he did succeed in blocking the most extreme isolationist measure to come before Congress in the entire interwar period. In 1935 Representative Louis Ludlow, an Indiana Democrat, had introduced a constitutional amendment to require a popular referendum before Congress could declare war. The Ludlow referendum reflected the fear of many isolationists that a president could lead a frightened Congress into war against the wishes of the majority of the people. When Ludlow was unable to secure consideration for his proposal in the House Judiciary Committee, he filed a discharge petition, which required the signa-

---

[6]Winston Churchill, *The Gathering Storm* (Boston, 1948), p. 254.

tures of a majority of the House of Representatives (219 Congressmen) to permit action on his amendment. Until the spring of 1937 Ludlow was unable to win many supporters. But when the permanent Neutrality Act was passed, isolationists and pacifist pressure groups focused their support on the Ludlow referendum. The lobbying activity quickly produced results. Gallup polls in the fall of 1937 showed that seven out of every ten Americans believed that Congress should be compelled to obtain the approval of the people before declaring war. By early December Ludlow had secured the signatures of 205 Congressmen, and when the Japanese attacked the *Panay*, he gained the thirteen more that he needed. The House leaders accordingly scheduled debate on a resolution to consider the war referendum for January 10, 1938.

The Ludlow amendment posed a serious challenge to the administration. A number of public figures had come out in opposition to the scheme—Henry L. Stimson, Walter Lippmann, and Alfred M. Landon, the defeated Republican presidential candidate in 1936. Roosevelt did not reveal his own views until a press conference on December 17 when he sharply denounced the war referendum. Hull also publicly objected to the amendment, warning that it would "seriously handicap" the conduct of foreign policy and "impair disastrously" the government's efforts to keep the peace.[7] Privately, the administration worked feverishly to persuade Democrats who had signed the discharge petition to reverse themselves when the vote was taken in the House. When the debate took place on January 10, 1938, the House leaders went all-out. Floor leader Sam Rayburn delivered an impassioned plea against "this most tremendous blunder"; William Bankhead left the Speaker's chair to read a letter to his colleagues from Franklin Roosevelt warning that the amendment "would cripple any President in his conduct of our foreign relations."[8] These remarks, together with Postmaster-General Farley's telephone calls threatening to cut off patronage from recalcitrant

[7] *The Memoirs of Cordell Hull* (2 vols; New York, 1948), I, 564.
[8] *Congressional Record*, January 10, 1938, pp. 277, 281.

Democrats, proved effective; the House voted 209 to 188 against consideration of the amendment.

The slender margin by which Congress avoided acting on the Ludlow amendment highlighted the obstacles confronting Roosevelt in his desire to alter the course of American foreign policy. By risking his prestige in a showdown, he had prevented the isolationists from undermining his control of American diplomacy. But negative achievements were all he could secure. The nation was stalled at dead center — torn between the paralyzing fear of war, as reflected in the strong support for the Ludlow referendum, and the dawning realization that world events menaced the United States, as shown by the unexpected praise of the Quarantine speech. But the nation continued in its passive role, reacting to events abroad rather than shaping viable alternatives in a troubled world.

II

For two years after the reoccupation of the Rhineland in March 1936, Hitler abstained from outright aggression in Europe. He had secretly sent aid to the Spanish Rebels, joined with Japan in the Anti-Comintern Pact, and formed the Rome-Berlin Axis, but he had not sought any additional territory nor made any provocative demands. Yet during these two years German power had grown immensely. The rearmament publicly announced in 1935 began to reach its peak in 1938, with the major emphasis on producing the offensive weapons developed during World War I — tanks, airplanes, and submarines. Britain had only begun extensive expansion of its war production in 1937 and the French continued to concentrate on the Maginot Line, the huge complex of fixed fortifications begun in 1930 that stretched along the German frontier from Switzerland to Belgium. Equally important, France and especially Great Britain under Neville Chamberlain, who became Prime Minister in April 1937, were committed to a defensive foreign policy. They were willing to accept German grievances at face value and search for means of satisfying each new demand that Hitler put forward. At times Chamberlain and Edouard Daladier, the Radical-Socialist who became Premier of France in 1938, seemed to anticipate Hitler's desires and offered to make concessions to demands that Germany had not yet even formulated.

Hitler was ready to take advantage of this favorable situation. In a conference with his chief advisors on November 5, 1937, he indicated the future course of German foreign policy. First, he stressed the necessity of reuniting all Germans into a greater Third Reich. In particular he intended to annex Austria, the Sudeten area of Czechoslovakia with its three and a half million Germans, and the city of Danzig. Then Hitler spoke in vague and grandiose terms of the need for *Lebensraum* — living space — for the greater Germany he planned to create. Rejecting both the idea of expanding trade through normal commercial channels and amassing a great colonial empire, Hitler said the food and raw materials the new Germany would require demanded expansion to the east, to the non-German areas of Poland and the Ukraine. This second goal would lead inevitably to war with the Soviet Union, and was thus to be subordinated to the more immediate aim of creating the expanded Germany at the expense of Austria, Czechoslovakia, and Poland. Hitler planned to mask this aggression in the cloak of Wilsonian self-determination, claiming that he intended only to right the wrongs of Versailles by giving all Germans in Europe the chance to live under German rule.

The first step in the new Pan-German policy came in March 1938, when Hitler provoked a crisis in Austria. With German troops poised on the Austrian frontier, Kurt von Schuschnigg resigned as Chancellor in favor of a leading Austrian Nazi. In a radio address to his people, Schuschnigg explained that he had yielded to the threat of force. "We are not minded at any price to shed German blood," he asserted, and then concluded, "God save Austria!"[9] In the early hours of the next morning the new Chancellor invited Hitler to send German troops into Austria to prevent violence and bloodshed. By

[9]Whitney H. Shepardson, *The United States in World Affairs, 1938* (New York, 1939), p. 39.

mid-day on March 12 the German army had moved into Vienna without firing a shot, and at four in the afternoon Hitler himself crossed the frontier in a triumphant return to the land of his birth. The *Anschluss* of Germany and Austria, forbidden in the Versailles settlement, was an accomplished fact.

The world watched silently while Hitler began his drive to dominate Central Europe. On the night Austria committed national suicide, France was caught in a cabinet crisis that left her without a government. In Britain Neville Chamberlain explained to the House of Commons that the close relations and the ethnic ties between the German and the Austrian peoples made the *Anschluss* inevitable, although he personally disapproved of the veiled use of force. The United States kept studiously quiet, but on April 6 the State Department tacitly recognized the German achievement by transforming the American legation in Vienna into a consulate. Four days later Hitler conducted plebiscites in Germany and Austria to approve of the union of the two countries. With Nazi storm troopers supervising the election, voters in Austria outdid their German neighbors by marking 99.75 per cent of the ballots affirmatively. *Anschluss* was now complete.

The entire world soon became aware that Czechoslovakia was Hitler's next target. In the spring of 1938 the leader of the Sudeten Germans was demanding complete autonomy for his three and a half million people in this region of Czechoslovakia bordering on the Third Reich. The Czechs refused, and turned to France and England for support. The French had made a firm treaty commitment to aid the Czechs against attack by a third power, but France would not act without the cooperation of Great Britain. The Soviet Union also was committed to aid Czechoslovakia, but this pledge depended on prior action by France. Thus the fate of Czechoslovakia rested with Britain, who was not bound by any treaty obligations to give aid or support against German aggression.

In early September 1938 negotiations between the German minority in the Sudeten and the Czech government had reached an impasse. Ready to grant autonomy to the German group, the Czech leaders now found that Hitler would settle for nothing less than the cession of the Sudetenland to Ger-

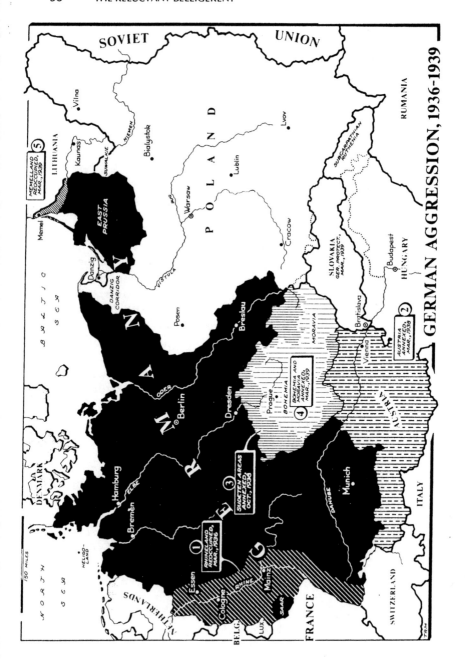

GERMAN AGGRESSION, 1936-1939

many. Unlike the Austrians, the Czechs had a well-equipped army entrenched in extensive fortifications in the Sudeten Mountains. Realizing that the continued existence of Czechoslovakia as a nation was at stake, President Eduard Beneš appealed to France for assistance. The French immediately turned to Britain, and on September 15 Neville Chamberlain journeyed to Hitler's mountain retreat at Berchtesgaden to seek a solution to the crisis. In a three-hour interview Hitler demanded that the Czechs cede the Sudeten territories to Germany. Chamberlain took this extreme demand in stride, and after consultations with the French he informed President Beneš on September 19 that Czechoslovakia must surrender all territory in which Germans were in the majority. Two days later Beneš agreed to these humiliating terms, which involved the loss of the strategic fortifications as well as 800,000 Czechs to Germany.

Chamberlain returned to Germany on September 22 to inform Hitler of the Czech surrender only to find Hitler now insisted on the immediate transfer of the territory in question. Chamberlain finally left Germany with a demand from Hitler that the Sudeten area be turned over by October 1 or his armies would march. French, British, and Czech public opinion stiffened in the face of German arrogance; Americans felt the threat of war with a deep shudder of fear, and at the height of the crisis Roosevelt lent his prestige in an effort to preserve peace. In a telegram to Hitler, Chamberlain, Daladier, and Beneš on September 26, the President urged further negotiations to achieve "a peaceful, fair and constructive settlement of the question at issue."[10] The next day Roosevelt followed up this appeal with a personal message to Hitler calling for a new conference of the European leaders in a neutral European capital. But at no time did Roosevelt suggest that the United States be represented at such a meeting, and he was careful to tell Hitler, "The Government of the United States has no political involvements in Europe, and will assume no obligations in the conduct of the present negotia-

---

[10]Department of State, *Peace and War: United States Foreign Policy, 1931-1941* (Washington, 1943), p. 246.

tions."[11] When Roosevelt learned that Chamberlain had finally accepted an invitation from Hitler to attend a conference at Munich to settle the Czech crisis, he immediately sent off a two-word cable: "Good man."[12]

The Munich Conference, held on September 29 and 30 between Hitler, Chamberlain, Daladier, and Mussolini, marked the climax of appeasement. In return for Hitler's promise not to seek an additional foot of territory in Europe, Britain and France agreed that Germany should occupy the Sudeten area in four stages between October 1 and October 7, leaving the final disposition of a fifth zone to an international commission. The Czechs agreed to the terms on the morning of September 30, and thus became the sacrifical victims of the worldwide demand for peace at any price.

The role of the United States in the Munich crisis was insignificant. Although a few charged that Roosevelt had been responsible for driving Chamberlain back to the conference table and surrender, all the evidence indicates that the British Prime Minister followed his own counsel. But there can be little doubt that the passive nature of American policy contributed indirectly to the outcome of the Munich Conference. Roosevelt's blunt statement to Hitler that the United States would not involve itself in European affairs was a green light to the German dictator to continue pressing Britain and France to abandon Czechoslovakia. It is also evident that the Roosevelt administration was relieved by the peaceful end of the crisis. In a radio address to the nation on October 3, Under Secretary of State Sumner Welles declared that the present moment offered the best chance in two decades to establish "a new world order based upon justice . . . and law."[13] Two days later Roosevelt sent a private message to Chamberlain which echoed these words: "I fully share your hope and belief that there exists today the greatest opportunity in years for the establishment of a new order based on justice and on law."[14] If

[11]*Ibid*, p. 429.
[12]*Foreign Relations: 1938*, I, 688.
[13]State Department, *Press Releases*, XIX (October 8, 1938), 240.
[14]Roosevelt to Joseph P. Kennedy, October 5, 1938, quoted in William L. Langer and S. Everett Gleason, *The Challenge to Isolation, 1937–1940* (New York, 1952), p. 35.

the United states was not directly responsible for the Munich settlement, the government had clearly placed its official seal of approval on this tragic event. American isolation had become the handmaiden of European appeasement.

III

The Munich Conference marked the high tide of American isolationism in 1930s. The initial relief at the avoidance of war soon passed, and when Americans took a second look at the Munich settlement, they began to doubt the wisdom of appeasing Hitler. Though 59% of those surveyed by the Gallup poll approved of Munich at the outset, by November nine out of ten Americans believed that Hitler intended to seize more territory in Europe. President Roosevelt shared this fear. His ambassador in France, William Bullitt, reported in early October that the French government now viewed Munich as a disastrous defeat for Britain and France. When Hitler confirmed this estimate by stepping up German rearmament, Roosevelt called for an additional expenditure of $300 million for national defense. American dislike of Germany was further intensified in early November with Hitler's new wave of vicious persecutions of Jews throughout Germany. Roosevelt responded by calling back Hugh Wilson, the American ambassador in Berlin, for consultation. When brutal German anti-Semitism continued, Roosevelt refused to send Wilson back to Germany, and from that time forward a *chargé d'affaires* represented the United States in Berlin.

Increased armaments and a diplomatic snub did not alter the passive role of the United States. After Munich, the Roosevelt administration considered revising the Neutrality Act of 1937. When the State Department asked Senator Pittman for his views, he suggested that Congress repeal the arms embargo and place all trade, including weapons, under cash-and-carry regulations. After considerable debate, State Department experts recommended that the administration adopt Pittman's suggestion and press for repeal of the arms embargo in the next Congress.

In his annual message to Congress on January 4, 1939, the President raised the issue of neutrality revision in a cautious and oblique fashion. Dwelling for some time on international problems, he warned that the forces of aggression loose in the world menaced the security of the United States. Roosevelt then stated cryptically, "There are many methods short of war, but stronger and more effective than mere words, of bringing home to aggressor governments the aggregate sentiments of our own people." He then turned to neutrality legislation, commenting that "our neutrality laws may operate unevenly and unfairly — may actually give aid to an aggressor and deny it to the victim."[15] He stopped short of any specific recommendations, but both isolationists and internationalists interpreted the speech as a call for revision of the neutrality legislation.

Roosevelt now faced the problem of securing drastic changes in the Neutrality Act from Congress. His own political power and prestige were at an all-time low. After his overwhelming reelection in 1936, the President had met with a series of political reversals. The attempt to pack the Supreme Court alienated many Southern conservatives in his party; the sharp recession in 1937 and 1938 weakened his popularity; and the unsuccessful purge of conservative Democrats in the party primaries in 1938, followed by sweeping Republican gains in the Congressional elections, cast real doubt on his ability to lead the nation. A frontal assault on neutrality legislation which still enjoyed widespread public and Congressional support might be disastrous. When Senator Pittman offered to take charge in Congress, Roosevelt jumped at the opportunity to shift the burden. Although Pittman had authored the previous neutrality acts and had at times expressed views similar to those of Senator Nye, Roosevelt felt that he had to gamble on the questionable leadership of the Nevada Senator.

For the next two months Pittman procrastinated. Meanwhile a group of internationalists led by Clark Eichelberger of the League of Nations Association devised their own form of

[15]Samuel Rosenman, ed., *The Public Papers and Addresses of Franklin D. Roosevelt* (13 vols.; New York, 1938-1950), VIII, 1-3.

neutrality revision which Senator Elbert D. Thomas of Utah agreed to sponsor in Congress. The Thomas amendment, introduced in the Senate on February 13, proposed to grant the President power to embargo the export of all war supplies, raw materials as well as arms, to belligerents. However, the President, with the consent of Congress, would be able to lift this total embargo for victims of aggression if a nation went to war in violation of its treaty obligations. Although the Thomas amendment, which was designed to align the United States behind Britain, France, and China, won enthusiastic approval from leading internationalist spokesmen, Roosevelt remained silent, refusing to comment on neutrality revision at his press conferences.

Adolf Hitler finally broke the deadlock on neutrality legislation on March 15, 1939. At six in the morning the German army marched into Czechoslovakia in a flagrant violation of the Munich agreement. Franklin Roosevelt shared the indignation that swept the nation and now concentrated on the Neutrality Act. "If Germany invades a country and declares war," he told Senator Tom Connally of Texas, on March 16, "we'll be on the side of Hitler by invoking the act."[16] The next day he broke his long silence on neutrality revision, telling a press conference that prompt action was imperative. Pittman belatedly began working in earnest on the legislation in a series of conferences with State Department experts, who did most of the actual drafting. The measure, which Pittman grandly labeled the Peace Act of 1939, provided for the repeal of the arms embargo and the placing of all trade with belligerents on a cash-and-carry basis.

In a radio address to the American people, Senator Pittman argued that his proposal would prevent American involvement in foreign war while guaranteeing American aid to England and France because of their control of the sea. Isolationists attacked the proposal on precisely the same grounds, warning that aid to the Allies would eventually lead to American entry into war in the 1940s just as it had in 1917. At the other ex-

[16]Tom Connally and Alfred Steinberg, *My name is Tom Connally* (New York, 1954), p. 226.

treme, the supporters of the Thomas amendment criticized Pittman's proposal because it would favor Japan and penalize China in the Far East, a feature which the Chinese government quickly pointed out to the State Department. Roosevelt was so unhappy over this obvious inequity that at one point he wrote Hull that the cash-and-carry plan "works all wrong in the Pacific. The more I think the problem through" he continued, "the more I am convinced that the existing Neutrality Act should be repealed *in toto* without any substitute."[17] Pittman finally introduced a separate resolution to permit the President to embargo exports to any country violating the Nine Power Treaty as a way to prevent the Japanese from benefiting from cash-and-carry. This obviously discriminatory proposal, which the State Department approved, revealed the true intent of neutrality revision. Although the administration advocated cash-and-carry in order to preserve the superficial appearance of impartial neutrality designed to keep the United States out of war, the real aim was legislation that would extend American aid to the likely victims of aggression. It would have been far more honest, and perhaps even more expedient, for the administration to have come out clearly for the Thomas amendment, and fight for a policy of all-out opposition to aggressors.

The introduction of the Pittman resolution encouraged the administration. The long delay now seemed over, and the fact that the cash-and-carry provisions of the 1937 Act were due to expire on May 1 was an additional incentive for prompt Congressional action. But once again Pittman disappointed Hull and Roosevelt. When the Senate Foreign Relations Committee met in early April, he submitted to pressure from members of the Committee to hold lengthy hearings on neutrality revision. For weeks a steady stream of witnesses appeared before a handful of Senators in the large caucus room of the Senate Office Building. Internationalists, isolationists, advocates of cash-and-carry, and upholders of traditional international law repeated familiar arguments, boring the committee members

[17]Roosevelt, ed., *F.D.R. Letters*, II, 873.

and the sparse audience. The most notable feature of the hearings was the surprisingly large number of witnesses who spoke in favor of the Thomas amendment. "No trade with treaty-breakers," they demanded, as they insisted that the United States must align itself against aggressors in order to prevent the outbreak of world war.

As the hearings droned on, it became clear that while the majority of the American people were not ready to discriminate against aggressors, they did favor the repeal of the arms embargo. In February 1939 the Gallup poll showed virtually an even division of opinion on this question, but after the German seizure of Czechoslovakia in March, 66% of the people queried favored repeal. Although this percentage dropped slightly, throughout the spring the polls revealed a clear majority favoring neutrality revision along the lines of the Pittman bill. Despite this favorable public climate, Senator Pittman continued to procrastinate. On May 1 the cash-and-carry provisions of the 1937 Act expired with the Senate Foreign Relations Committee still mired down in the hearings. Finally, in mid-May Pittman informed Cordell Hull that he planned to postpone further consideration of neutrality for several weeks. "The situation in Europe," Pittman wrote, "does not seem to induce any urgent action on neutrality legislation."[18] By this time both Hull and Roosevelt realized that they had backed the wrong horse in the Senate, and they decided to shift their attention to the House of Representatives, where Sol Bloom, Chairman of the Foreign Affairs Committee, was eager to sponsor neutrality revision. On May 19 the President invited Bloom to attend a conference at the White House with House leaders and Secretary of State Hull. At this meeting Roosevelt stressed the need for repeal of the arms embargo to prevent war in Europe, or at least to make a victory for "the powers unfriendly to the United States" less likely if war did come."[19] Stressing the crucial nature of the arms embargo, the Presi-

---

[18]Pittman to Hull, May 16, 1939, Papers of the Senate Committee on Foreign Relations, File 76A — F9, National Archives.
[19] *Hull Memoirs*, I, 643.

dent indicated that he had no objection to the cash-and-carry formula. He did express the hope that the House would act promptly, preferably by July 12, when the King and Queen of England were due to visit the United States.

This conference at the White House marked a significant turning point in the long struggle for neutrality revision. After four months of inaction with Pittman, Roosevelt had openly committed the administration to the principle of repeal of the arms embargo. He did not, however, want to enter the debate personally. Thus instead of issuing a Presidental appeal for legislation, he had Cordell Hull state the administration's position in a letter to Pittman and Bloom which was made public on May 27, 1939. In this letter, Hull called for repeal of the arms embargo and the adoption of a modified cash-and-carry system for all trade with belligerents. Pointing out that modern war had erased the distinction between munitions and raw materials, Hull maintained that the administration's proposal would "make easier our twofold task of keeping this nation at peace and avoiding imposition of unnecessary and abnormal burdens upon our citizens."[20]

Congressman Bloom quickly framed a neutrality resolution which carried out the desires of the administration and steered it successfully through the House Foreign Affairs Committee, in early June. When the resolution cleared the Committee, the administration exerted intense political pressure on the House to secure a favorable vote. Hull met with small groups of Congressmen in his private apartment; the President spoke out forcefully for revision at his press conference on June 20; State Department officials presented the case at a meeting of the Democratic steering committee on June 19.

When debate began on June 27 on the floor of the House, administration spokesmen were confident they could pass the Bloom resolution. Although there was intense opposition from isolationist Congressmen, who called the bill "Un-American," "immoral and un-Christian," and "a brazen attempt of interventionists to involve us into the international racket of finance and munitions manufacturing," prospects for passage

---

[20]State Department, *Peace and War*, p. 464.

seemed very strong.[21] But then late in the evening of June 29, Representative John M. Vorys of Ohio rose and proposed a major amendment to restore the embargo on arms and ammunition, though not on implements of war. The House rejected this proposal on a show of hands, but when a vote by tellers was taken at the request of the isolationists, the amendment passed, 159 to 157. By a two-vote margin, the House had voted to restore the arms embargo that the administration was trying to remove. The next day the Democratic leaders tried to strike the Vorys amendment from the Bloom resolution, but they were defeated by four votes, 180 to 176. The House then went on to pass the legislation which failed to do more than slightly modify the existing arms embargo.

The administration had suffered a resounding defeat. At a press conference the next day Cordell Hull voiced his disappointment. President Roosevelt kept silent, though he did reveal his feelings to a Democratic Congresswoman from New York who had voted for the Vorys amendment. "I honestly believe that the vote last night was a stimulus to war," he wrote, "and that if the result had been different it would have been a definite encouragement to peace."[22] Roosevelt was not ready to give up the quest for repeal of the arms embargo. Having failed in the House, he returned to the Senate, asking Pittman to convene the Senate Foreign Relations Committee and report out the cash-and-carry measure. Twice Pittman postponed committee meetings, but finally his group met on the morning of July 11. There were twenty-three Senators present. Eleven were certain to vote for neutrality revision; ten were opposed to it. Two Democratic Senators, Walter F. George of Georgia and Guy M. Gillette of Iowa, were uncommitted. Neither was a staunch isolationist, but both were bitter political enemies of the President who had survived Roosevelt's attempts to purge them from the party in the 1938 primaries. When Senator Pittman called the Foreign Relations Committee to order, Senator Bennett Clark immediately moved that

[21]*Congressional Record*, June 27, 1939, p. 8017; *ibid.*, June 28, 1939, p. 8152; *ibid.*, June 29, 1939, p. 8249.

[22]Roosevelt, ed., *F.D.R. Letters*, II, 899–900.

they postpone consideration of neutrality legislation until the next session of Congress in 1940. Senators George and Gillette supported the motion, ensuring its adoption, 12 votes to 11. The committee then adjourned. In fifteen minutes it had totally nullified six months of effort by the administration.

Roosevelt was thoroughly angered by the action of the Senate Foreign Relations Committee. He prepared a message to Congress in which he planned to denounce the isolationists, but Hull finally persuaded him to follow more conciliatory tactics. On July 14 the President sent Congress a long statement on neutrality prepared by Hull which argued calmly and judiciously for repeal. Calling upon Congress to reconsider its stand on neutrality revision, Hull warned that the arms embargo "encourages a general state of war" and therefore "its results are directly prejudicial to the highest interests and to the peace and security of the United States."[23]

Roosevelt followed up this message by calling a conference of Senate leaders at the White House on the evening of July 18. A half dozen Senators from both parties joined the President, Secretary Hull, and Vice-President John Nance Garner in the second-floor study. In this informal atmosphere Roosevelt shared his concern for the state of the world with the Senators and pleaded for repeal of the arms embargo. When Cordell Hull backed up the President's remarks by citing the alarming reports received daily from American diplomats abroad, Senator Borah challenged the accuracy of this intelligence, asserting that he did not believe war was likely to break out soon in Europe. "I have my own sources of information which I have provided for myself," declared Borah, "and on several occasions I've found them more reliable than the State Department." Hull realized that further argument was useless. Garner quietly went around the room to canvass the views of those present, and then bluntly told Roosevelt, "Well, Captain, we may as well face the facts. You haven't got the votes, and that's all there is to it."[24]

[23]*Congressional Record*, July 14, 1939, p. 9128.
[24]Joseph Alsop and Robert Kintner, *American White Paper* (New York, 1950), pp. 58-59.

The next day the White House issued a brief press release blaming the Senate for the postponement of neutrality revision. The Senate was responsible for failing to act decisively on the critical issue of neutrality, although President Roosevelt's inept handling of this issue contributed to the outcome. Fearful that personal engagement in the neutrality debate would only lose the support of those he had antagonized on domestic issues, the President had stayed in the background, allowing first Pittman and later Hull to lead the administration drive for revision. Pittman proved to be an incompetent leader; Hull lacked the prestige and personal magnetism of the President. Only Roosevelt could have dramatized the issue and awakened the broad public response necessary to spur Congress into action. Such an effort might not have been successful; Senator Nye and others threatened a filibuster that might have blocked revision even if the House and the Senate Foreign Relations Committee had acted favorably. Yet if Roosevelt had risked his prestige by entering into the thick of the debate, he might have overcome this stubborn resistance. He at least could have had the satisfaction of knowing that he had made a supreme effort to use American influence to prevent war in Europe.

IV

The German seizure of Czechoslovakia in March ushered in a new period of rising tension in Europe. Prime Minister Chamberlain and the British people were shocked by Hitler's perfidy. Realizing that Poland was the next German objective, on March 30 Chamberlain offered the Polish government an ironclad guarantee that Britain and France would give assistance if Germany attacked. Hitler responded to this sudden shift in British policy by denouncing the German-Polish non-aggression treaty of 1934 and the Anglo-German Naval treaty of 1935. The era of appeasement had ended. For the first time since the rise of Hitler, England and France appeared willing to run the risk of war to halt further German expansion in Europe.

The Soviet Union now held the key to the European situation. The Anglo-French guarantee to Poland was totally unrealistic from a military standpoint. If Germany invaded Poland, the Western allies could not render direct assistance to the Poles, and given the ineffective striking power of the armies on the western front, they would even be unable to relieve Poland by invading Germany. To make their commitment effective, they would have to win over the Soviet Union, whose armies could move into Poland and fight against Germany. Yet the Russians were suspicious of Britain and France. They viewed the Munich Conference as a deliberate betrayal of Russian security, and they had no confidence in the determination of Britain and France to stand firmly against Hitler. Nevertheless, Stalin was willing to begin negotiations with the British and French in the summer of 1939 to explore the possibility of an alliance against Hilter. British and French military and diplomatic missions went to Moscow, but the talks proved fruitless. Mutual suspicion, coupled with the fact that Poland feared Russian assistance almost as much as German aggression, led to the collapse of these negotiations by mid-August.

The impasse between the Soviets and the Western Allies provided Adolf Hitler with an opportunity which he boldy exploited. Trade talks had been in progress between Germany and Russia since late May. In early August the German ambassador in Moscow raised the question of a political agreement between the two countries. When the Soviets responded favorably, intense negotiations between Germany and Russia ensued. On August 20 the two countries signed a commercial agreement. Three days later, Joachim von Ribbentrop, the German Foreign Minister, flew to Moscow and signed a non-aggression pact with Russia. The Nazi-Soviet Pact, which caught Britain and France completely by surprise, was a deceptively simple document. It merely provided that the two nations would refrain from aggression against each other, and would remain neutral if either became involved in war with other countries. There was, however, a secret protocol by which Germany recognized Finland, Latvia, Estonia, and the eastern half of Poland as part of the Russian sphere of influence. For Hitler, this seemed a small price to pay for the freedom to dispose of western Poland without fear of Russian interference.

The signing of the Nazi-Soviet Pact led to the outbreak of war in a week's time. It is by no means certain that Hitler planned or expected a major European war to develop in 1939. He was still dealing with the men of Munich, and he probably believed that England and France would now back down and permit him to destroy the independence of Poland. It was this miscalculation on Hitler's part that made war inevitable. On August 25 Britain responded to the Nazi-Soviet Pact by signing a formal treaty of alliance with Poland to back up the guarantee that Chamberlain had given in March. Last minute negotiations continued between Germany and England, but unlike the previous year the British government turned its back on appeasement. Hitler, continuing to believe that the Western allies would not honor their commitments, went ahead with his plans to invade Poland. On the morning of September 1 the German blitzkrieg began. Two days later Britain and France sent separate ultimatums to Germany, and when Hitler refused to halt his armies, both nations declared war. The Second World War, which people had been predicting since the mid-1930s, became a reality.

The outbreak of war in Europe led to swift and far-reaching changes in American foreign policy. Germany's lightning thrust through Poland, destroying that nation in a few weeks' time, shocked the American people into realizing that what happened in Europe was of real and immediate concern to them. Now that England and France were locked in battle with Nazi Germany, a strong wave of sympathy for the Western allies swept over the United States. The belief in disinterested neutrality nurtured so carefully in days of peace became one of the first casualties of the war, and the Roosevelt administration quickly discovered that the issue of neutrality revision, so bitterly fought in the spring, now had strong popular support. Torn between their conflicting desires to remain at peace and yet to have Hitler defeated, the American people saw in neutrality revision the opportunity to aid England and France without risking involvement in the European conflict.

On the evening of September 3, after the British and French

declarations of war, President Roosevelt spoke to the American people in a fireside chat. He stressed his dedication to keep America at peace, but warned that the war was bound to affect the United States. "When peace has been broken anywhere," he told his audience, "peace of all countries everywhere is in danger." Moreover, unlike Wilson in 1914, he did not ask that the American people be impartial. "This nation must remain a neutral nation," he declared, "but I cannot ask that every American remain neutral in thought as well . . . Even a neutral cannot be asked to close his mind or his conscience."[25] The President then waited two days before issuing the formal proclamation of American neutrality and invoking the provisions of the 1937 Act.

Roosevelt's words to the American people and his delay in proclaiming neutrality revealed his distaste for the rigid legislation he was compelled to invoke. On the day that Germany attacked Poland he had decided to ask Congress to repeal the arms embargo, but he moved cautiously, fearful of provoking the isolationists. Throughout the first week of September he carefully canvassed the views of Congressional leaders in an attempt to assess the mood of the nation. At a press conference on September 8 Roosevelt announced that he planned to call Congress back into special session in order to repeal the arms embargo. His soundings of public opinion encouraged him, and on September 11 he wrote Neville Chamberlain, "I hope and believe that we shall repeal the embargo next month and this is definitely a part of the Administration's policy."[26] Two days later the President issued the formal call for Congress to reassemble on September 21. Fully aware of the importance of the issue, he abandoned his cautious policy of the preceding spring and prepared to risk his prestige in an all-out effort to revise the neutrality legislation. Despite favorable public opinion, he knew that the isolationists would oppose him bitterly and that it would take all of his political skill to secure repeal of the arms embargo from a suspicious Congress.

The President and his White House staff worked overtime to build up solid majorities in Congress. Lists of the Democratic

[25]Rosenman, ed., *Public Papers of Roosevelt*, VIII, 460-63.
[26]Roosevelt, ed., *F.D.R. Letters*, II, 919.

Representatives who had voted for the Vorys amendment in the spring were compiled and pressure was applied to these men. Eager to win the support of southern Democrats who opposed him on domestic issues, he asked Senators Tom Connally of Texas and James Byrnes of South Carolina to assist Pittman in guiding neutrality revision through the Senate. Nor did the President neglect Republicans; when such prominent businessmen as Thomas W. Lamont, a partner in J. P. Morgan and Company, and Myron Taylor, former chairman of the board of U.S. Steel, offered their support in lining up favorable votes in Congress, Roosevelt was delighted. In order to make repeal a nonpartisan campaign, he invited Alfred M. Landon and Colonel Frank Knox, the unsuccessful Republican candidates in 1936, to attend a White House conference with congressional leaders from both parties on September 20. Although this conference proved disappointing, Landon and Knox came out strongly for repeal, and the Republican leaders in Congress announced that they would not treat neutrality revision as a partisan issue.

At noon on September 21 President Roosevelt entered the House chamber to address the special session of Congress. In slow, measured tones he grimly reviewed the events that had led to war in Europe. Announcing that he now regretted having signed the original Neutrality Act in 1935, he called on Congress to return to "the ancient precepts of the law of nations" by repealing the arms embargo. Although he did not specifically call for the enactment of cash-and-carry provisions, he recommended that American citizens, American ships, and American property be kept out of the combat zones. Asserting that such a program offered "far greater safeguards than we now possess or have ever possessed to protect American lives and property from danger," he closed by reaffirming his determination to keep the United States out of war.[27]

It was a brilliant political speech. Appealing constantly to his desire to return to traditional international law, Roosevelt never even hinted that his proposals would link the United States with England and France against Germany. By insisting

[27]*Congressional Record*, September 21, 1939, pp. 10-12.

that his recommendations would better protect the nation from involvement in war, he sought to undermine isolationist opposition. Although most contemporary journalists and commentators divined that Roosevelt's true motive was to aid England and France, Roosevelt set the tone for the ensuing debate. For the next six weeks the administration would carry on the elaborate pretense that the sale of arms to the Allies was but the accidental by-product of a program designed solely to keep the United States out of war.

While Congress considered the President's proposals, a fierce public debate began between the supporters and opponents of neutrality revision. In mid-September a group of isolationists, led by Senators Borah, Nye, and La Follette, formed a "peace bloc" to arouse the American people and defeat the drive to repeal the arms embargo. Borah commenced this publicity campaign on September 14 with a nationwide radio address in which he argued that the adminstration, motivated by a desire to aid England and France, was taking the first step toward intervention in the European war. The next night Charles A. Lindbergh, the aviator-hero of the 1920s who had avoided public life since the tragic kidnapping of his son in 1932, called upon the American people to hold fast to the policy of isolation. These radio appeals gave rise to a tremendous deluge of Congressional mail demanding the retention of the arms embargo. In three days a million pieces of mail arrived in Washington, with letters favoring the arms embargo outnumbering those opposed by a ratio of 100 to 1. Isolationist peace societies organized mass rallies to stir up further public opposition to repeal, while such diverse individuals as Norman Thomas and Herbert Hoover joined Lindbergh in radio appeals to the American people. The popular response to these pleas indicated that isolationism was far from dead in the United States, and many Congressmen began to reconsider their stand on the arms embargo in the face of this intense emotionalism.

Concerned by the isolationist outcry, President Roosevelt quietly sought to counter it by asking Clark Eichelberger, director of the American Union for Concerted Peace Efforts, the group which had sponsored the Thomas amendment in the spring, to organize a committee to rally public opinion to the cause of repeal. Eichelberger agreed, and in late September he persuaded William Allen White, the widely respected Republican newspaper editor from Kansas, to head a Non-Partisan Committee for Peace through Revision of the Neutrality Act. The White Committee, as it soon became known, came into being on October 2 when several hundred prominent educators, businessmen, writers, clergymen, and civic leaders agreed to work for repeal of the arms embargo. Throughout October this committee sponsored radio addresses by such prominent Americans as White, Alfred E. Smith, and Henry L. Stimson, and carried on an effective campaign for repeal at a grassroots level through local units in thirty states. By the end of the month, the efforts of the White Committee had offset the isolationist drive against appeal and had achieved nationwide support for the President's program.

While the public debate raged, Senator Pittman met with the Democratic members of the Foreign Relations Committee and drafted the administration's neutrality measure. On September 26 the full Senate committee reported out the bill by a partisan vote of 16 to 7. Four Democrats who had opposed repeal of the arms embargo in July voted for the measure, while all but one Republican on the committee voted against it. The Pittman bill called for the repeal of the arms embargo, but in every other respect it adhered to the concept of strict neutrality. The most significant feature was a rigid cash-and-carry section which required that title to all exports to belligerents be transferred before the goods left the United States and that they be carried in foreign ships. Thus shipments to such areas as Hong Kong, Australia, and South Africa would be treated in exactly the same manner as exports to England and France. The President was given authority to ban the entry of American citizens, ships, and aircraft into combat zones that he might designate. The bill continued the ban on passenger travel on belligerent ships and the prohibition on loans to governments at war contained in the 1937 Act. Thus Pittman, in an obvious effort to placate isolationist sentiment, proposed to limit executive authority to an irreducible minimum. The price for repeal of the arms embargo would be the sacrifice of the American merchant marine, which would be denied the right to trade with British and French possessions throughout the world.

The Senate began consideration of the Pittman bill on October 2. For the next three weeks there was a deluge of oratory as seventy Senators spoke on the measure. From the outset the administration was confident of ultimate success, and the Democratic leaders, following the curt advice of Vice President Garner "to keep their mouths shut," permitted the isolationists to dominate the debate.[28] Pittman, Connally, and Byrnes, who spoke for the administration, simply described the terms of the bill and argued that it was designed solely to prevent American involvement in the war by keeping American ships and American citizens off the high seas. Despite constant harassment from opponents of the measure, the administration spokesman refused to admit any partiality toward the European belligerents. Tom Connally summed up their stand when he declared, "We are trying to keep out of war—not get closer to it."[29]

The isolationists refused to accept this explanation. In the opening speech against the bill, Senator Borah charged that the only purpose of the measure was to assist England and France. Repeal, he asserted, was "an act of intervention." Others echoed this charge for the next three weeks. Selling arms to England was but the first step toward war, claimed the isolationists—next would come American money, and finally American troops. Challenging the sincerity of the administration spokesmen, the opponents of the bill endorsed the cash-and-carry proposals, but asked why they could not have the arms embargo as well. Expressing a sincere fear of involvement, the isolationists pleaded for a continuation of the existing legislation. "In the long run," declared Senator Arthur Vandenberg of Michigan, "I do not believe that we can become an arsenal for one belligerent without becoming a target for another."[30]

It became increasingly evident that the majority of the Senators favored repeal of the arms embargo. Meanwhile, American commercial interests exerted intense pressure on the administration to relax the cash-and-carry restrictions. Responding to these appeals, the State Department drew up an amendment limiting the cash-and-carry restrictions to the North Atlantic, Asia, and the Pacific. Pittman fought this concession, but finally permitted it to be presented to the Senate, which quickly adopted it.

The Senate debate ended on October 27. Over a million words had been spoken, but it is doubtful that the oratory changed a single vote. After rejecting an amendment to restore the arms embargo, the Senators proceeded to pass the Pittman bill by a vote of 63 to 30. Senators from the Northeast and the South favored the bill by overwhelmingly large margins; most of the negative votes came from the Middle and Far West.

The Pittman bill then went to the House, where the outcome was in doubt. Remembering the defeat in the spring when the Vorys amendment slipped through by a few votes, Roosevelt had Postmaster General Farley and Vice President Garner work on recalcitrant Democrats. William Allen White made a personal appeal to the House Republicans, telling Minority Leader Joseph Martin, "I would hate to have my party put itself in a posture where it can be charged that we play Mr. Hitler's game in the matter of the embargo."[31] These tactics proved successful. After a brief three-day debate, the House voted to repeal the arms embargo, 243 to 181. The overwhelming support of Southern Representatives, who voted 110 to 8 in favor of repeal, gave the administration its margin of victory.

A little before noon on November 4, 1939, a beaming Franklin Roosevelt signed the Neutrality Act of 1939 as news-

[30]*Ibid.*, October 4, 1939, p. 96.
[31]Walter Johnson, ed., *Selected Letters of William Allen White* (New York, 1947), p. 399.

BELLIGERENT AND COMBAT ZONES 1939

BOUNDARIES ARE THOSE OF 1937

Combat areas prohibited to American shipping

Belligerent coasts prohibited to American shipping

American ships permitted to proceed to belligerent coasts south of this line

reel cameras recorded the historic scene. He handed the two pens he had used to sign the legislation to Senator Pittman and Representative Bloom, and then issued a proclamation declaring the North Atlantic a combat zone. No American ship could enter the area from Spain to the Baltic even if destined for a neutral port. The restrictions on loans and travel in the 1937 Act remained in force. But now, for the first time since the outbreak of war, American citizens could sell arms, ammunition, and implements of war to the European belligerents provided that title was transferred before the munitions left the United States and that they were carried away in foreign ships. In theory Germany could buy arms from the United States, but British control of the sea meant that only England and France would benefit from this change in American neutrality legislation. Once again, the United States was destined to become the arsenal of democracy.

The repeal of the arms embargo was hailed as a great victory in England and France. The British press called it "A Smashing Blow to Germany," while Neville Chamberlain wrote Roosevelt that the action was "a profound encouragement to us in the struggle upon which we are engaged."[32] Despite the rhetoric of impartiality cultivated by Roosevelt and by Congressional advocates of repeal throughout the debate, neutrality revision was intended to aid England and France. The tide of isolationism that ran through the 1930s had reached its peak in 1938. The Munich Conference, the destruction of Czechoslovakia, and the invasion of Poland had led to a growing awareness that German aggression in Europe imperiled the security of the United States in the Western Hemisphere. Ties of culture and ideology with England and France reinforced the increasing fear of German power and weakened the earlier conviction that the United States could remain aloof from the European maelstrom.

The repeal of the arms embargo thus marks a crucial turning point. The isolationists had warned that such a step would lead inevitably to American entry into the war, and they were

[32]New York *Times*, October 28, 1939, p. 1; *Foreign Relations: 1939*, I, 681.

right. Few Americans yet conceived of the awesome military potential of Nazi Germany; even those who sympathized with England and France believed that modest American aid would suffice to bring about the defeat of Hitler. Americans still clung to the illusion that the United States could protect its security by measures short of war.

CHAPTER IV

Taking Sides

T HE FIRST FEW MONTHS of the Second World War bewildered most Americans. In September German armored divisions overran Poland with amazing ease. Hitler achieved this brilliant victory by leaving the western front undermanned, but the French, outnumbering the German forces facing them by more than two to one, limited themselves to a cautious advance into the Saar basin. Before they could mount a more ambitious offensive thrust, resistance in Poland had disintegrated and Germany had reinforced her troops in the west. Soon both sides had built up strength to the level of one hundred divisions, but neither Germany nor the Western allies were willing to undertake a major offensive before the onset of winter. Thus there ensued a war of nerves in which both sides confined activity to routine patrols and occasional air raids dropping leaflets rather than bombs.

The war at sea was only slightly more active. The powerful British Navy swept German commerce from the world's oceans and instituted a blockade to cripple the German economy. Hitler had neglected to build up the submarine fleet on which Germany had relied so heavily in World War I, and during the first few months of the conflict German U-boats inflicted only minimal damage on Allied shipping. Even the vexing issues of neutral rights that had troubled the United States so deeply from 1914 to 1917 failed to emerge. German submarine commanders were instructed to avoid attacking American ships at all costs. In the first two months of the war, before the cash-and-carry policy removed American commerce from the combat zone in Europe, not a single American ship was torpedoed. Despite a few critical voices over the British blockade of Germany, the State Department confined itself to polite protests and legal reservations in its correspondence with the British Foreign Office.

Throughout this period of "phony war," the Roosevelt administration made every possible effort to insulate the United States from the European conflict. When Hitler made peace overtures in October, President Roosevelt remained aloof, not wishing to offer his services as a mediator in arranging a peace that would grant Germany the fruits of aggression. The major American diplomatic initiative was designed to keep the war out of the Western Hemisphere. In early September Cordell Hull arranged for Panama to call for a meeting of the foreign ministers of the American states to adopt common policies toward the European war. On September 23 representatives of the twenty-one republics met at Panama City, with Under Secretary of State Sumner Welles representing the United States. After eight days of consultation the foreign ministers approved sixteen declarations to insure that the Western Hemisphere would remain an island of peace in a world at war. The most significant act, the Declaration of Panama, created a hemispheric neutrality belt for three hundred miles out to sea around both North and South America, with the exception of Canada. This novel edict, which was Roosevelt's own brainchild, warned the belligerents not to engage in naval activity within this zone, and authorized the American states to patrol the neutrality belt with their navies and report any infractions. None of the European belligerents acknowledged the legality of the neutrality zone, and throughout the war German submarines and British surface vessels violated it repeatedly. Nevertheless, the United States Navy did patrol for 300 miles out into the North Atlantic, and, as the war progressed, cooperated with Great Britain in combating German submarine activity within this zone. Thus the hemispheric policy, like most American measures in this period, revealed the distinctly pro-British cast of American neutrality.

The Soviet Union broke the stalemate in Europe and aroused the American people in the fall of 1939. In mid-September Soviet armies moved into Eastern Poland to claim the area that Germany had assigned Russia in the secret protocols of the

RUSSIAN EXPANSION, 1939

ARCTIC   OCEAN

NORTH CAPE

Petsamo

Murmansk

Narvick

WHITE SEA

Archangel

GULF OF BOTHNIA

FINLAND

NORWAY

LAKE LADOGA

SWEDEN

Helsinki

Oslo

Leningrad

GULF OF FINLAND

Stockholm

ESTONIA

S O V I E T

BALTIC SEA

LATVIA

Moscow

DENMARK

Memel

LITHUANIA

AREAS ACQUIRED BY
THE SOVIET UNION
IN 1939

Danzig

EAST
PRUSSIA

Minsk

Bremen

Berlin

U N I O N

Berlin

P O L A N D

G E R M A N Y

Kiev

BOHEMIA

SUDETEN-
LAND

MORAVIA

SLOVAKIA

AUSTRIA

BESSARABIA

HUNGARY

RUMANIA

Odessa

ITALY

YUGOSL.

500 MILES

BLACK
SEA

TRM

Nazi-Soviet Pact. Russia absorbed these provinces, which possessed a heavy Ukrainian and White Russian population, and then applied diplomatic pressure on the Baltic States. In October Latvia, Estonia, and Lithuania agreed to allow Russian troops to occupy bases on their soil, a step which led to the incorporation of these countries into the Soviet Union within the next year. Russia then turned to Finland, which was included within her sphere of influence by the Nazi-Soviet Pact; Stalin, intent on bolstering Russian defenses against Germany, demanded that the Finns cede territory on the Karelian Isthmus, only twenty miles from Leningrad, and on the Arctic sea near the ice-free port of Petsamo, as well as permit Russia to lease the harbor of Hangö and nearby islands in the Gulf of Finland. In return, Stalin proposed to cede some remote forested areas to Finland.

The Finnish government entered into negotiations with the Soviet Union, but it quickly became apparent that Finland would fight rather than submit to this diplomatic blackmail. On November 29 Vyacheslav Molotov, the Russian Foreign Minister, denounced the Finns in a long radio harangue, and the next morning the Soviet Union invaded Finland without declaring war. Finland had won the esteem and respect of the American people by continuing to pay its debt in the 1930s when all other European nations defaulted. Long-standing American dislike and distrust of the Soviet Union, coupled with the obvious Russian aggression, led to virtually unanimous sympathy for Finland in the United States. Isolationists and internationalists praised Finland's struggle "for all of Western civilization" and condemned the "ruthless savagery" and "sheer brutality" of the Soviet Union.[1] Herbert Hoover abandoned his usual aloof stance to become chairman of a Finnish Relief Fund, though he bewildered the Finns by refusing to allow the money raised to be used for military supplies. And Hoover must have been surprised to find that his allies in this cause included Colonel Robert McCormick, Secretary of the Interior Harold Ickes, and Fiorello LaGuardia, the fiery mayor of New York who declared that "democracy is on the

[1]Robert Sobel, *The Origins of Interventionism: The United States and the Russo-Finnish War* (New York, 1960), p. 79.

side of Finland, civilization is on the side of Finland, and Finland is on the side of God."[2]

The spontaneous public support for Finland was embarrassing to Roosevelt and Hull. Both men deplored the Soviet aggression, but did not want to drive Stalin into Hitler's arms. They believed that the Nazi-Soviet pact was a frail bond between incompatible totalitarian systems, and they wished to do everything possible to bring about a break between Germany and Russia. Consequently, Roosevelt had not publicly condemned the Russian seizure of Eastern Poland, nor had he applied the Neutrality Act to the Soviet Union for her partnership with Germany. When he learned that the Soviet Air Force had bombed the city of Helsinki, the President did issue a public statement denouncing "this new resort to military force" and he appealed to American aircraft manufacturers to halt the export of planes and aircraft parts to the Soviet Union.[3] But he carefully avoided invoking the Neutrality Act, and when the Finnish ambassador requested military aid, he politely declined.

The intital stages of the "Winter War" revealed surprisingly strong resistance by the Finns and remarkable inefficiency by the Russians. The spectacle of little Finland holding off the Soviet Union rallied American opinion to the aid of Finland. Senator Prentice Brown, a Michigan Democrat who normally voted as an isolationist, introduced a bill to permit the Reconstruction Finance Corporation to loan $60 million to Finland for nonmilitary purposes. Roosevelt, under pressure to refund the latest installment of the Finnish debt repayment, neatly dodged the issue. In a message to Congress on January 16, 1940, the President stated that he had put the money into a special account, and that "the matter of credits to the Republic is wholly within the jurisdiction of the Congress. . . ."[4]

Congress reluctantly acknowledged its responsibility and proceeded to pass a bill increasing the capital of the Export-Import Bank by $100 million and authorizing a maximum loan of $20 million to Finland, provided that no money be

[2]*Ibid.*, p. 80.
[3]New York *Times*, December 2, 1939.
[4]*Ibid.*, January 17, 1940.

used to buy munitions. Even this modest measure was hotly debated, and it passed by rather slim margins. By the time the act went into effect in March, the Soviet offensive had broken the resistance of the Finnish army. On March 13 Finland signed the Treaty of Moscow, surrendering to Russia the entire Karelian Isthmus, several islands in the Gulf of Finland, and a large expanse of territory in the north. Finland had lost 25,000 square miles of territory; 12 per cent of her population was uprooted. The United States had played an equivocal role in the "Winter War," expressing extravagant sympathy for the plight of the Finns but offering little actual help. The need to prevent a break with the Soviet Union, a potential ally against Hitler, had outweighed moral considerations. Such a policy was logical, but one can understand the feelings of the Finnish Foreign Minister when he remarked in mid-March that American sympathy was so great that "it nearly suffocated us."[5]

A similar pattern of public sympathy and cautious administration policy characterized the American stand toward the war in the Far East. The Japanese had occupied the most populous and productive areas of China in 1938 and 1939, controlling the coastal region and all the major ports. Stubborn resistance by the Chinese Nationalists frustrated the Japanese plan to liquidate the war in China and move on to new exploits. The United States continued to condemn Japanese aggression, but the administration confined its protests to flagrant Japanese violations of the rights of American citizens in China. Although Roosevelt approved a loan of $25 million to Chiang Kai-shek in December 1938, there was no effort to stop the steady flow of scrap iron and oil to Japan. Thus while the government extended modest financial aid to China, private American exporters supplied the raw materials vital to the Japanese war effort.

In 1939 American public opinion became increasingly hostile to Japan. The American Committee for Non-Participation in Japanese Aggression, headed by Henry L. Stimson, mounted a very effective campaign against the export of oil

[5]William L. Langer and S. Everett Gleason, *The Challenge to Isolation, 1937–1940* (New York, 1952), p. 340.

and scrap iron to Japan; a poll taken in the summer indicated that 82 percent of those surveyed favored the prohibition of the sale of war supplies to the Japanese. The idea caught on in Congress, and in June and July of 1939 a series of resolutions were introduced to restrict trade with Japan. Secretary of State Cordell Hull, fearful that embargoes would lead to war, opposed these resolutions. To offset this movement he finally decided to accept an idea advanced by Senator Arthur H. Vandenberg, Republican isolationist spokesman from Michigan, to give Japan the required six months notice that the United States was terminating the commercial treaty of 1911 between the two countries. When the six months were up, the United States would be legally free to institute restrictions on commerce with Japan. Hull hoped that this maneuver would quiet the public discontent without leading to a showdown.

The outbreak of war in Europe resolved Hull's dilemma. The hostilities across the Atlantic captured the attention of the American people and thus eased the pressure for embargoes in the Far East. Japan also became preoccupied with the European conflict and its implications. Japanese leaders, who had been angling for an alliance with Germany against Russia, were stunned by the Nazi-Soviet Pact; and in the months of confusion and indecision that followed, they were not prepared to challenge American abrogation of the commercial treaty of 1911.

Throughout the fall of 1939 the State Department wrestled with the problem of American Far Eastern policy. Ambassador Joseph Grew, who had been in Japan since 1932, was in Washington on a furlough, and he pressed repeatedly for a policy of accommodation, urging that the United States ease its opposition to Japan's ambitions in the Far East and negotiate a new commercial treaty as part of an overall settlement with Japan. Hull, outraged by the aggression in China and fully aware of public antagonism to Japan, rejected Grew's advice. Unwilling either to appease or challenge Japan, Hull finally persuaded Roosevelt that the United States should continue a modest policy, upholding American rights in China without risking war with Japan.

On January 26, 1940, when the commercial treaty of 1911 expired, the State Department informed Japan that trade would continue on a day-to-day basis. Henry Stimson protested vigorously in a letter to the New York *Times*, and his committee renewed its efforts to curb trade with Japan. But the administration held firmly to its new policy. Hull was not ready to force a crisis with Japan, but he hoped that the ever-present threat of trade embargoes would serve as a brake on Japanese expansion. "I was careful to give them no enlightenment," he later wrote. "I felt that our best tactic was to keep them guessing. . . ."[6]

The cautious policy of the United States toward both Japan and the Soviet Union in the early months of the European war indicated the Roosevelt administration's belief that Germany posed the major threat to American security. Despite the public indignation expressed over the plight of Finland and China, Roosevelt and Hull refused to take action that might restrict their freedom to move against Hitler in the future. The American people were not yet ready to go beyond the mild cash-and-carry aid to Britain and France, but their leaders were already looking forward to more active measures in Europe. Passive acceptance of the "dreadful rape of Finland," as the President termed it privately, and a diplomatic holding action against Japanese aggression, were the price that Roosevelt was willing to pay to insure that the United States would contribute to the destruction of Nazi Germany.[7]

I

The "phony war" came to an end on April 9, 1940. In a single day Hitler's forces occupied Denmark and the southern portion of Norway. Britain and France, preparing to meet a German offensive in Northern France, were caught completely by surprise. The British rushed an expeditionary force to Norway, but these troops were unable to dislodge the Germans

[6]*The Memoirs of Cordell Hull* (2 vols.; New York, 1948), I, 638.
[7]Elliott Roosevelt, ed., *F.D.R.: His Personal Letters, 1928–1945* (2 vols.; New York, 1950), II, 961.

and were soon withdrawn. This stunning failure toppled Neville Chamberlain from power, and on May 10 Winston Churchill formed a new government in England to take charge of the war against Hitler.

The Scandinavian campaign was only the prelude to the all-out German offensive in the West. On May 10, Hitler unloosed his panzer divisions on the neutral countries of Belgium and the Netherlands. Armored columns supported by dive bombers knifed through the defenses of the low countries; in five days the Dutch were compelled to surrender. The British forces in France rushed into Belgium to stop the onslaught only to fall into the trap Hitler had laid. On May 14 German tanks broke through the French lines near Sedan and sped toward the English Channel. In less than a week German forces had reached the sea at Abbéville, cutting off the entire British expeditionary force as well as many scattered units of the French army. In desperation, the English troops raced for the port of Dunkirk. Despite the surrender of Belgium on May 28, the British were able to carry out a miraculous evacuation of their forces before Dunkirk fell on June 4. Nearly 350,000 soldiers escaped from the German trap, but this remarkable achievement should not obscure the fact that Germany had dealt the Allies a shattering defeat. In three weeks Hitler had conquered Belgium and the Netherlands, driven the British off the continent, and had his armies poised to destroy a demoralized France. By using modern weapons in a bold and novel way, Germany had achieved a revolution in the art of war which imperiled the security of every nation in the world.

On the day that Dunkirk fell, Churchill delivered a stirring speech to the House of Commons; he reiterated his determination to fight on even if Germany conquered the British Isles "until, in God's good time, the New World, with all its power and might steps forth to the rescue and liberation of the old."[8] This veiled reference to eventual salvation by the United States was echoed in France. On June 5 Germany resumed its offensive against the ill-equipped and ill-led remnants of the French army. Six days later, with the advance German units ap-

[8]Winston S. Churchill, *Blood, Sweat and Tears* (New York, 1941), p. 297.

proaching Paris, Prime Minister Paul Reynaud sent a personal telegram to Franklin D. Roosevelt asking him to give England and France "aid and material support by all means 'short of an expeditionary force.'" Promising that such aid would not be in a lost cause, Reynaud pledged: "We shall fight in front of Paris; we shall fight behind Paris; we shall close ourselves in one of our provinces to fight and if we should be driven out of it we shall establish ourselves in North Africa to continue the fight and if necessary in our American possessions."[9]

A few hours before he received Reynaud's appeal, President Roosevelt spoke out bluntly at Charlottesville, Virginia, on the tragic events in Europe. In an address to the graduating class at the University of Virginia, Roosevelt ridiculed the policy of isolation and made clear his attitude toward the European struggle. "Overwhelmingly we, as a nation," the President proclaimed, "are convinced that military and naval victory for the gods of force and hate would endanger the institutions of democracy in the Western World, and that equally, therefore, the whole of our sympathies lies with those nations that are giving their life blood in combat against these forces." He then denounced Italy, which earlier that day had declared war against France. "On this tenth day of June, 1940, the hand that held the dagger has struck it into the back of its neighbor."[10] Roosevelt concluded by promising to send to England and France all available material aid in their struggle against Hitler and Mussolini.

When Roosevelt received Reynaud's telegram, there was little more that he could say. He released the French plea for help to the public, and on June 13 he sent a reply to Reynaud encouraging him to fight on in North Africa if Germany overran France. Meanwhile, French resistance continued to crumble. Paris fell to the German forces and the government fled to the south. On July 14, Reynaud delivered a final appeal to Roosevelt. "The only chance of saving the French nation, vanguard of democracies, and through her to save England, by whose side France could then remain with her powerful navy,"

[9]Department of State, *Peace and War: United States Foreign Policy, 1931–1941* (Washington, 1943), pp. 549, 550.
[10]*Ibid.*, pp. 547, 548.

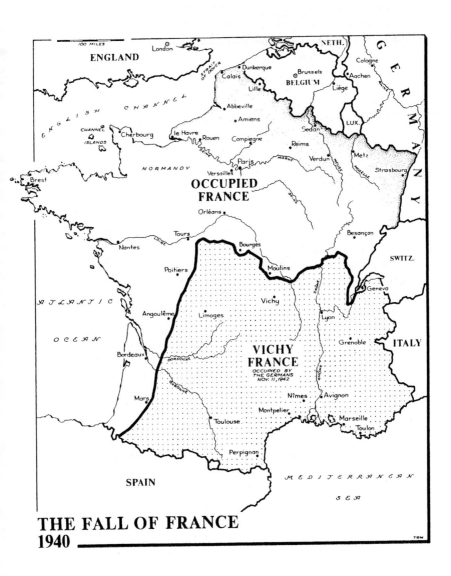

THE FALL OF FRANCE
1940

Reynaud pleaded, "is to throw into the balance, this very day, the weight of American power."[11] Sorrowfully, Roosevelt replied the next day. He told Reynaud that he admired the courage of France; that he would make every effort to send additional supplies to England and France; that he would not recognize the legality of the German conquest of France; but that he could not commit the United States to military intervention in the war. "Only the Congress," Roosevelt concluded, "can make such commitments."[12] Three days later Marshal Pétain replaced Reynaud as head of the French government and surrendered his country to Germany. Hitler was now master of Western Europe.

The great German blitzkrieg, culminating in the fall of France, transformed American attitudes toward the war in Europe. The months of military inaction had bred a complacency and cynicism which now gave way to a sense of urgency and intense concern. In January, 1940, Roosevelt had asked Congress to appropriate slightly less than $2 billion for national defense, a modest increase over the previous year. For the next three months, economy-minded Congressmen whittled away at the Presidential request in committee. A week after the German thrust into Belgium and Holland, President Roosevelt went before Congress to ask for an additional billion dollars to strengthen the nation's security. An alarmed Congress acted with amazing speed; in late May both Houses approved additional appropriations of one-and-a-half billion, and when Roosevelt sought another billion on May 31, Congress granted this sum in two weeks' time. Heartened by this sudden cooperation, the President sent in a request for nearly $5 billion on July 10 to meet the new situation created by the fall of France. In September Congress approved this expanded program, raising the total defense appropriations in 1940 to $10.5 billion. Fearful of the peril to American security from a victorious Germany, Congress had voted a five-fold increase in expenditures for national defense.

The changing American attitude toward the European war found expression in the formation of the Committee to Defend

[11]*Ibid.*, p. 552.
[12]*Ibid.*, p. 553.

America by Aiding the Allies. William Allen White and Clark Eichelberger, the men responsible for organizing public support for the repeal of the arms embargo, became worried over the complacency of the American people in the spring of 1940 and they met to consider creating a new committee to arouse the public. When Hitler unleashed his great offensive in May, they decided it was time to act. On May 17 White sent a telegram to several hundred prominent American men and women. "As one democracy after another crumbles under the mechanized columns of the dictators," White declared, "it becomes evident that the future of western civilization is being decided upon the battlefield of Europe. . . . The time has come when the United States should throw its material and moral weight on the side of the nations of western Europe great and small that are struggling in battle for a civilized way of life."[13] White asked the recipients of his telegram to join with him in appealing to the American people for increased aid for the Allies. Within an hour enthusiastic replies began flowing in from clergymen, university presidents, and distinguished public leaders from all walks of life. Heartened by this response, on May 20 White made public the existence of the committee and formally launched an intensive publicity campaign to convert the American people to the cause of all-out aid to England and France.

The White committee was an immediate success. Within six weeks over 300 local chapters were formed representing every state except North Dakota. Small donations from the rank and file financed the work of the committee, though there were larger contributions from such diverse individuals as J. P. Morgan and David Dubinsky, president of the International Ladies Garment Workers Union. White, who continued to edit his newspaper in Emporia, Kansas, supervised the overall policy of the committee, but the larger task of organization and day-by-day direction was carried on by Clark Eichelberger in New York City, where the committee had its headquarters. Eichelberger employed every possible technique of public pressure to advance the viewpoint of the committee. Local chapters sent petitions, telegrams, and letters to the President

---

[13]Walter Johnson, *The Battle Against Isolation* (Chicago, 1944), p. 69.

and Congress; the committee sponsored national radio broadcasts and mass rallies in major American cities; Robert Sherwood, the noted playwright, prepared a dramatic full-page
advertisement, "Stop Hitler Now," which appeared in news-
papers around the nation in early June.

The activities of the White Committee, together with the
ominous news from Europe, led to startling changes in American attitudes. During the winter months the great majority of
the American people saw no reason to extend aid to England
and France, and perceived little danger to the United States
from the fighting in Europe. In a poll taken just after the outbreak of the war, 82% of those surveyed believed that England
and France would defeat Germany. In May, when the blitzkrieg began, a majority still foresaw an eventual Allied
victory. But with the fall of France this confidence was shattered; now a majority answered that Germany was likely to win
the war. This new estimate made most Americans receptive to
the campaign of the White Committee for additional aid to
England. In a poll taken in June, four out of five Americans
questioned favored giving Britain more material support. And
they realized where this aid might lead; in a poll in June 65%
of those replying thought that the United States would enter
the war before it was all over. Yet despite the fear of a German
victory, the desire to aid England engendered by the White
Committee, and the belief in eventual involvement, the great
majority of Americans clung to the policies of neutrality and
isolation. In June 1940 82% opposed entry into the European
conflict. Shaken by the German victories, the American people were willing to back the administration in a policy of all-
out aid to Britain, but they insisted that this aid stop short of
war.

II

In the summer of 1940 Americans watched tensely as the
Battle of Britain began. Lacking the naval strength to launch
an immediate invasion of England, Hitler decided to subdue
the British from the air. On July 10 the German *Luftwaffe* be-

gan a series of heavy bombing raids on British shipping and ports along the English Channel. In mid-August Hitler shifted the attack to airfields in southern England, hoping to destroy the R.A.F. Meanwhile, German submarines, now operating out of French ports, began an increasingly effective campaign against British shipping. In May the British lost only 75,000 tons of shipping, but in June the losses totaled 290,000 tons. Using wolfpack techniques, the German submarines penetrated British convoys and threatened to sever Britain's lifeline to the United States and the Empire. Under attack from the air and the sea, Britain's chances for survival seemed tragically slim to many Americans. For the first time in their lives, many realized that England was indeed America's first line of defense. If Germany was able to invade the British Isles and take the British Navy intact, the Atlantic would be transformed from a secure barrier into a broad highway for German penetration of the Western Hemisphere.

The United States could do little to help the British meet the attack from the air, but there were measures the Roosevelt administration could take to assist the war at sea. On May 15, 1940, Winston Churchill had asked Roosevelt to give Britain 40 or 50 over-age destroyers for convoy duty. Britain had begun the war with 100 destroyers in her home waters; by May nearly half had been lost. The United States had over 200 destroyers dating back to World War I. The United States Navy commissioned 172 of these vessels for active duty, but it could spare enough to meet the British request. President Roosevelt was fearful that every available ship might be needed to protect the Atlantic approaches to the United States, and hesitated to fulfill Churchill's request. Moreover, Congress had decreed in the naval expansion bill of June 28 that the President could not transfer military equipment to a foreign country until the Chief of Naval Operations certified that it was "not essential to the defense of the United States."[14] This legal obstacle worried Roosevelt. Mainly he feared the reaction of Congressional isolationists if he sanctioned such a clear-cut violation of neutrality. Roosevelt was planning to run for a

[14]*Statutes at Large,* LIV, 681.

third term and he did not wish to provide the Republicans with a campaign issue. Thus in his reply to Churchill, the President explained the difficulties he faced and promised only to give the matter further thought.

Despite a personal plea from King George, Roosevelt continued to procrastinate through June and July. At a meeting with William Allen White on June 29, Roosevelt outlined the problem and stressed the obstacles to a transfer of the destroyers. White felt that Roosevelt had "lost his cud," and he decided to have the Committee to Defend America by Aiding the Allies agitate on this issue in order to strengthen the President.[15] Throughout July and August, the White Committee focused its energies on the destroyer issue, encouraging members to write to the President urging the transfer, sponsoring mass rallies, and printing newspaper advertisements with the bold headline, "Between Us and Hitler Stands the *British* fleet!"[16] The Committee's most effective move came on August 4 when it sponsored a radio broadcast by General John J. Pershing, the American commander in World War I. "America will safeguard her freedom and security by making available to the British or Canadian governments at least fifty of the over-age destroyers, which are left from the days of the World War," Pershing declared. "If the destroyers help save the British fleet, they may save us from the danger and hardship of another war."[17]

While the White Committee stimulated nationwide support for transfer of the destroyers, a faction inside the Committee, known as the Century group, met to consider how they could persuade Roosevelt to act. The Century Group consisted of businessmen, lawyers, journalists, and intellectuals, primarily in New York City, who wanted to go beyond the moderate policy of the White Committee and advocate American entry into the war. Alarmed by the inaction on the destroyer issue, these men decided to approach the President with a novel suggestion — the United States would turn over 50 destroyers to Eng-

[15]Johnson, *Battle Against Isolation*, p. 100.
[16]*Ibid.*, p. 100.
[17]*Ibid.*, p. 102.

land in return for bases on British possessions in the Western Hemisphere and a pledge by Britain never to surrender its fleet to Germany. On August 1 a three-man delegation presented the proposal to Roosevelt. The President listened noncommitally, but the next day he discussed the idea with his cabinet and decided to explore this possibility with the British.

The Century group had broken the logjam on the destroyer issue, but a month of tedious negotiation followed before the deal could be completed. Fearful of political opposition, the President insisted that the Republican candidate, Wendell Willkie, approve the transaction. William Allen White undertook this delicate mission, and after some early difficulty was finally able to report to Roosevelt that Willkie would not attack the destroyer deal publicly. The British raised objections, preferring not to link the transfer of bases with the destroyer issue, but they finally acquiesced. The legal obstacle was overcome when the Chief of Naval Operations declared the destroyers surplus on the grounds that the acquisition of bases meant a net strategic gain for the United States. Finally, on September 2, 1940, Cordell Hull and Lord Lothian, the British Ambassador, completed the destroyers-for-bases transaction with an exchange of letters. The next day the President transmitted this executive agreement to Congress for its information. The same day Great Britain gave public assurances that it would never permit the British Navy to pass into German hands.

The destroyers-for-bases agreement marked the end of American neutrality. In giving 50 warships to Great Britain, the United States was openly declaring its support of England in the war against Germany. The acquisition of sites for eight naval and air bases in British possessions stretching from Newfoundland on the north to British Guiana on the south blunted the isolationist criticism, for if Roosevelt had not performed "the most important action in the reinforcement of our national defense that has been taken since the Louisiana Purchase," as he told Congress, he had clearly strengthened American security in the Atlantic.[18] But this achievement was

---

[18]State Department, *Peace and War*, p. 565.

totally inconsistent with the status of neutrality. From this time forward the United States was a nonbelligerent, not yet at war with Germany, but clearly aligned with Britain in the struggle against Hitler.

At the time Roosevelt was bitterly assailed by isolationists for undertaking such a momentous step without the consent of Congress. Yet there could be little question that his action met with the overwhelming approval of the American people. A public opinion poll revealed that 70% of the people supported the destroyer deal. Indeed, Roosevelt could easily be accused of acting too cautiously. He had procrastinated on Churchill's request at a time when the fate of England hung in the balance; he had allowed a group of private citizens to solve his dilemma; he had not acted until he had made certain that it was politically safe for him to do so. Roosevelt's hesitation had led William Allen White to warn him in June "you will not be able to lead the American people unless you catch up with them"[19] Moving too slowly for the internationalists and too swiftly for the isolationists, Roosevelt had carefully gauged the national temper before committing the country to a status of nonbelligerency. His moderation proved to be wise, for when he finally acted, he carried the nation with him. Roosevelt knew that the great majority of the American people were still torn between a desire to defeat Hitler and a determination to stay at peace. The destroyers-for-bases agreement came within the limits of this national consensus.

III

The sweeping German victories which ended American neutrality toward the European war also had a profound impact on American interests and policies in the Far East. The Japanese, entering into the fourth year of a seemingly endless campaign to conquer China, were astonished by the speed and completeness of the German success in Europe. Japanese militarists quickly perceived that the defeat of the Netherlands,

[19]Johnson, *Battle Against Isolation*, p. 82.

France, and Britain gave them a perfect opportunity to expand southward to Indo-China, Malaya, and the Dutch East Indies. Southeast Asia, with its vast reservoir of oil, rice, rubber, and tin, now lay exposed. The Japanese army could turn from the stalemate in China to win new glory by achieving the Greater East Asia Co-Prosperity Sphere so long heralded by Japanese propagandists. Only the United States stood between Japan and dominance of all Asia.

Japanese leaders moved swiftly to take advantage of the new power vacuum in the Far East. Their first objective was to end the aid reaching Chiang Kai-shek in the interior of China from the British and French in the south. On June 7, 1940, the day that France ended its resistance in Europe, the Japanese government demanded that the Vichy regime stop the flow of supplies over the railroad from Indo-China into South China. Three days later the French agreed, and the Japanese won the right to station inspectors in northern Indo-China to supervise the ban. Japan then demanded that Britain close the Burma Road, the other main supply line to China. The British, preparing to meet the German onslaught from the air, were in no position to resist, and in July Churchill agreed to close the highway for three months, much to the displeasure of American diplomats. Thus within a month after the fall of France, the Japanese had sealed off Chiang Kai-shek's forces from the outside world and were in a position to move into the virtually undefended areas of Southeast Asia.

Even those bold actions failed to please the militarists in Japan, and on July 16 a new government came to power under Prince Konoye, a popular but weak politician. The strong figures in the new cabinet were Yosuke Matsuoka, the Foreign Minister, and General Hideki Tojo, the Minister of War, both advocates of military expansion and a closer alignment with Hitler's Germany. In a series of crucial meetings on July 26 and 27, the Konoye cabinet agreed to pursue an aggressive foreign policy to reap the maximum rewards from the German successes in Europe. The primary objective was to continue the isolation of Chiang Kai-shek in order to complete the conquest of China. More ominous were the twin resolves "to foster a strong political tie with Germany and Italy" and to maintain "a firm front towards the United States" while exploiting the resources of Southeast Asia.[20]

The American response to the new Japanese challenge was slow in developing. The German blitzkrieg, the fall of France, and the Battle of Britain monopolized public attention in the spring and summer of 1940. After abrogation of the trade treaty of 1911 in January, there had been some agitation for embargoes against Japan, and two resolutions to this effect were introduced in Congress, but Hull successfully held out against such measures. President Roosevelt, however, did institute one significant change in American policy in the spring of 1940 as a warning to Japan. In April the American fleet, based in California, conducted maneuvers in the vicinity of the Hawaiian Islands. In early May, before the German offensive began in Europe, the President ordered the fleet to remain at Pearl Harbor indefinitely. Although the admiral in command protested against this shift in base, Roosevelt stuck by his decision, convinced that the presence of the fleet at Hawaii, on the flank of any Japanese thrust into Southeast Asia, would have a restraining effect on Japan.

Throughout the summer of 1940 President Roosevelt and his advisers agreed that Germany marked the major threat to American security, and in the Far East they were primarily concerned with preventing Japan from undertaking any drastic action that would affect Britain's ability to resist in Europe. The crucial issue was whether or not the United States should restrict the export of strategic materials, especially petroleum and scrap iron, to Japan. On this point Roosevelt's advisers were split. Secretary Hull and his associates in the State Department counseled against embargoes, fearful that economic pressure would provoke Japan into taking steps in Asia which neither Britain nor the United States could stop. Secretary of the Treasury Henry Morgenthau and Henry Stimson, who joined Roosevelt's administration as Secretary of War in June, disagreed. They argued that Japanese dependence on

[20]William L. Langer and S. Everett Gleason, *The Undeclared War, 1940–1941* (New York, 1953), p. 5.

the United States for scrap iron, and especially for oil, gave the nation an economic weapon which it had to use in order to prevent Japan from seizing all Southeast Asia. In this debate, which turned on conflicting estimates of the Japanese reaction to an embargo, Roosevelt leaned toward the State Department view, primarily because his military advisers warned that the nation was totally unprepared to wage war in the Pacific. Without proof that Britain could endure the German aerial onslaught and continue to guard the Atlantic approaches, the United States could only stand on the defensive in the Far East.

Proposals for an embargo of Japan had always been discussed in terms of a total cessation of trade in critical commodities, but in early July a new possibility developed. On July 2 the President signed the National Defense Act which contained a provision that had slipped through Congress without fanfare. The act authorized the President to restrict or even to prohibit entirely the export of any materials deemed essential to national defense. Advocates of economic pressure immediately realized the significance of this new power; the government could employ selective embargoes against Japan to reinforce diplomatic protests, without bringing on a rupture between the two countries. But when the President issued a list of forty critical materials under the terms of the new legislation, scrap iron and petroleum were conspicuously absent.

The advent of the Konoye cabinet and fear that Japan was embarking on a more aggressive policy brought reconsideration of the embargo issue toward the end of July. Stimson and Morgenthau stressed the importance of petroleum to the Japanese economy, and argued that an oil embargo would force the Japanese to moderate their policies. Hull disagreed, but during his absence from the capital, Morgenthau and Stimson persuaded the President to include all petroleum products and all scrap iron and steel in the list of materials essential for national security and hence barred from export. When Under Secretary of State Sumner Welles learned of this plan, he immediately protested, warning that it would mean war with Japan. The White House announced an embargo on these items on July 25, but the next day, after a heated discussion in the cabinet, Welles succeeded in limiting the embargo to aviation gasoline, rather than all petroleum products, and only the highest grade of scrap iron and steel. Despite this modification by the State Department, the July 26 order was a major departure in American foreign policy. Since the outbreak of the Manchurian incident in 1931, American officials had often discussed and rejected the idea of economic sanctions against Japan. Now the United States had finally embarked on the policy of economic pressure, and though the beginning was cautious and limited, it was a clear warning that the United States would no longer acquiesce in the creation of Japan's New Order in Asia.

The limited embargo, designed as a warning, came too late to influence the new Japanese government. On August 1 Japan began its movement south by demanding that France permit her to build a series of air bases in northern Indo-China and garrison troops there. The Vichy government tried to stall, while it pleaded with the United States for assistance, but by early September the French were compelled to agree in principle to the Japanese request. American officials, aware that the Japanese action in Indo-China was but the prelude to a long-range campaign to take over Southeast Asia, began a major reappraisal of American policy. In Tokyo Joseph Grew, who had consistently opposed sanctions and had advocated a policy of accommodation with Japan, reversed his position in a long cable to Hull on September 12. Warning that the German victories had, "like a strong wine," gone to the heads of Japanese statesmen, Grew classified Japan as a "predatory" power, "at every turn seeking to profit through the weakness of others." Affirming the preservation of the British fleet and the British empire as essential to American security, Grew reluctantly advocated the adoption of economic sanctions as a "show of force" to restrain the Japanese from further acts of aggression.[21]

Grew's message, the Japanese pressure on Indo-China, and rumors that Japan was about to sign a military alliance with

[21]State Department, *Peace and War*, pp. 569, 571-72.

Germany led to a major policy decision in Washington. On September 19 the cabinet discussed the situation. Morgenthau and Stimson pressed for embargoes on all petroleum and scrap iron exports, but Hull still resisted, reiterating his view that such a severe policy would provoke, not restrain Japan. The result was a compromise; the United States would embargo all shipments of scrap iron and steel, justifiable on grounds of national defense, but would not impose any additional restraints on the export of oil, which was far more important to the Japanese economy. This policy was to go into effect on October 16, but it was made public on September 24, after reports were received that the Japanese had concluded an agreement with the Vichy regime and had begun moving into Indo-China.

The embargo on scrap iron failed to satisfy the advocates of a vigorous policy. On September 23 Henry Morgenthau wrote in his diary, "My own opinion is that the time to put pressure on Japan was before she went into Indo-China and not after and I think it's too late and I think the Japanese and the rest of the dictators are just going to laugh at us."[22] It was too late. On September 27 the Japanese Ambassador to Germany signed a treaty of alliance with Germany and Italy in Berlin. In this Tripartite Pact the three powers agreed to respect each other's spheres of influence in Europe and Asia and undertook "to assist one another with all political, economic and military means when one of the three contracting Parties is attacked by a power at present not involved in the European War or in the Sino-Japanese Conflict."[23] To make it absolutely clear that the alliance was directed against the United States, a further clause specifically exempted the Soviet Union. In effect, Japan had joined with Germany in an effort to frighten the United States by raising the specter of a two-ocean war. The chief architect of the treaty, Japanese Foreign Minister Matsuoka, clearly stated the purpose of the alliance. "Germany wants to prevent American entry into the war," he told an Imperial

[22]Herbert Feis, *The Road to Pearl Harbor* (Princeton, 1950), p. 106.
[23]*Foreign Relations, Japan: 1931–1941*, II, 165-66.

Conference on September 26, "and Japan wants to avoid a war with the United States."[24]

The scrap iron embargo and the Tripartite Pact, both coming in late September 1940, revealed that Japanese-American relations had reached an impasse. Each nation had adopted a new and bold policy in hope of influencing and restraining the other. The Japanese had thrown in their lot with Germany to compel the United States to withdraw its opposition to Japanese expansion. This policy backfired. News of the Axis alliance stiffened the determination of American leaders to resist Japanese encroachments. What had once seemed to be a local threat in Asia now had become part of a worldwide danger to American security. The American people also reacted strongly, viewing Japan as the Asiatic branch of a conspiracy by the dictators to control the world. The American embargo policy was equally ineffective. The stoppage of scrap exports inconvenienced the Japanese but failed to cripple their war potential. It confirmed their decision to join with Nazi Germany and made them more sensitive than ever to their continued dependence on the United States for petroleum products. Even if the United States had embargoed oil, as Morgenthau wanted, it is doubtful if Japan would have been restrained. The oil which Japan needed was available in the Dutch East Indies, and the scrap embargo compelled the Japanese to begin laying plans to seize this vital area. An embargo on oil would simply have forced the Japanese to launch their assault on Southeast Asia in 1940, at a time when America was completely unprepared to defend the region.

The policies adopted by the United States and Japan in September 1940 made war between the two nations nearly inevitable. Each antagonist threatened the vital national interests of the other to the point where compromise was impossible. Japan could not accept any accommodation which denied her the opportunity to create a New Order in Asia; the United States could not agree to Japanese domination of Asia in cooperation with Nazi Germany at the expense of the British Empire. For the United States, this diplomatic deadlock was a se-

[24]Feis, *Road to Pearl Harbor*, p. 111.

rious defeat, for increased tension and the possibility of war in the Pacific conflicted with the basic American policy of all-out aid for Britain.

IV

By the end of the first year of the war, American foreign policy had undergone a startling transformation. The nation that had attempted to insulate itself from war was now committed to all possible aid to England and to economic pressure to restrain Japanese aggression in the Far East. Congress had taken some important steps, most notably in revising the Neutrality Act, voting increased defense expenditures, and approving of Selective Service in September, but the major policy decisions had been undertaken by the President. Both the destroyer-for-bases deal and the limited embargo on Japan were executive actions performed without the consent of Congress. Although public opinion polls showed that a substantial majority of Americans approved of these steps, the President was taking a very real gamble in an election year. The ultimate test would come in November with Roosevelt's bid for a third term in the White House.

The Republican party virtually ruled out a showdown on foreign policy when it chose Wendell Willkie, an outspoken supporter of aid to Britain, as its candidate in June, 1940. Willkie, a fiercely independent and rugged lawyer and utility executive from the Middle West, entered the Republican convention as a dark horse against such staunch isolationists as Senators Robert A. Taft and Arthur H. Vandenburg. But an astute political campaign waged by eastern Republicans, together with the sharp change in public mood after the fall of France, gave Willkie the nomination. The Republican candidate agreed with the administration's course of all-out aid to Britain, short of war, and contended only that he could conduct such a policy more adroitly than Roosevelt. By supporting both the destroyers-for-bases deal and the Selective Service Act, Willkie removed the major issues of foreign policy from the political arena.

Barred from the presidential contest, the isolationists found a way to present their views to the public during the election campaign. In the summer of 1940, R. Douglas Stuart, Jr., a Yale Law School student, and General Robert E. Wood, Chairman of the Board of Sears Roebuck and Company, formed a nationwide organization to counter the activities of the White Committee and place the isolationist viewpoint before the American people. On September 4, the day after the destroyer deal was made public, Stuart and Wood announced the creation of the America First Committee, with headquarters in Chicago. The response was immediately favorable. Local chapters sprang up throughout the Middle West and the Northeast, and soon America First was waging an intense propaganda effort. Officially a nonpartisan group, the America First Committee was heavily weighted toward the Republican party, and during the presidential campaign the radio speeches and newspaper advertisements it sponsored represented a major attack on Roosevelt's foreign policies.

The major theme of the America First movement was that all-out aid to Britain could end only in American entry into the European War. Their spokesmen skillfully probed at the glaring inconsistency of American opinion in 1940: the popular belief that material aid to England was sufficient to defeat a Germany powerful enough to be a direct menace to American security. The isolationists maintained that Hitler did not imperil the United States, that Britain and Germany were simply engaged in another round of the age-old struggle for the balance of power in Europe, and that "American democracy can be preserved only by keeping out of the European war."[25] Although the America First spokesmen were naive in their estimate of German strength, they made a valuable attempt to clarify the issues confronting the American people in 1940. If Hitler's Germany was as powerful and as ruthless as interventionists claimed, then both Willkie and Roosevelt were misleading the American people by asserting that the United States could maintain its security without entering directly into the war in Europe.

[25]Wayne S. Cole, *America First* (Madison, 1953), p. 15.

The candidates did little to clarify the issue raised by America First. Willkie began a vigorous campaign in early September, but he neglected foreign policy to hammer away at the third term issue. Roosevelt kept carefully aloof from politics until mid-October, giving only two speeches. In the first, to the Teamsters Union on September 11, he concentrated on domestic problems, but in one brief reference to foreign policy he proclaimed, "I hate war, now more than ever. I have one supreme determination — to do all that I can to keep war away from these shores for all time."[26] A month later, in a Columbus Day speech at Dayton, Ohio, the President was more forthright, warning the nation of the peril it faced from the aggressors overseas. On this occasion he proclaimed his determination to continue aid to Britain in the face of grave danger. "No combinaton of dictator countries of Europe and Asia," the President declared, "will stop the help we are giving to almost the last free people now fighting to hold them at bay."[27]

Roosevelt's conflicting statements, affirming his determination to keep the nation at peace while extending all possible aid to Britain, provided Willkie with an opening he could not resist. With his campaign going badly, he succumbed to the advice of party professionals and began an assault on Roosevelt's foreign policy. In speeches in late October Willkie questioned Roosevelt's sincerity in pledging to keep the nation out of war, and implied that the President had entered into secret understandings with the British. At Baltimore on October 30 he charged that if Roosevelt was returned to the White House, "you may expect we will be at war."[28] These accusations angered Roosevelt, and he responded by scheduling a series of speeches to set the record straight. In addresses in Philadelphia and New York, the President repeated the theme of his Teamster's speech, reaffirming his dedication to peace and ignoring the inconsistencies in the policy of all-out aid to Britain. Even these remarks did not reassure worried Democratic

[26]Samuel Rosenman, ed., *The Public Papers and Addresses of Franklin D. Roosevelt* (13 vols.; New York, 1938-1950), IX, 415.

[27]*Ibid.*, 466.

[28]Langer and Gleason, *Undeclared War*, p. 206.

leaders, and when the President traveled to Boston to deliver a speech to the predominantly Irish population, strongly isolationist because of antipathy toward England, he was under heavy pressure to make a final guarantee that he would not lead the nation into war. Reluctantly, Roosevelt agreed, and in Boston he declared:

And while I am talking to you mothers and fathers, I give you one more assurance.

I have said this before, but I shall say it again and again and again:

Your boys are not going to be sent into any foreign wars.

Even the Democratic platform had added the precautionary words, "except in case of attack," and when Roosevelt was reminded of this before the speech, he dismissed the omission with the comment, "Of course we'll fight if we're attacked. If somebody attacks us, then it isn't a foreign war is it?"[29]

"That hypocritical son of a bitch!" Willkie exclaimed when he learned of FDR's Boston speech. "This is going to beat me!"[30] The Republican candidate was right. A week later the American people returned Roosevelt to the presidency by a margin of 5 million votes. The third term issue, growing disenchantment with the New Deal, and Willkie's colorful personality had held Roosevelt to a modest victory compared to the landslide in 1936. But F.D.R. still won nearly 55% of the votes, and he could claim that he had a mandate from the people for his foreign policies. Although Roosevelt carefully equivocated on the crucial issue of aid to Britain and eventual involvement in the war, all interested parties interpreted the reelection of the President as a clear sign that the United States would continue to oppose Germany and Japan, even at the risk of war. Isolationists mourned; interventionists were jubilant. From England Winston Churchill commented that the election was "a message from across the ocean of great encouragement and good cheer."[31] If Roosevelt had failed to

[29]Robert Sherwood, *Roosevelt and Hopkins* (New York, 1948), p. 191.

[30]Ellsworth Barnard, *Wendell Willkie: Fighter for Freedom* (Marquette, Mich., 1966), p. 258.

[31]Langer and Gleason, *The Undeclared War*, p. 210.

clarify the ambiguity that continued to underlie American foreign policy, at least he had not misled the American people. They knew that they were moving down the road toward war; like their President, they moved reluctantly, hoping for a last-minute reprieve.

CHAPTER V

To the Brink

O N DECEMBER 2, 1940 President Roosevelt left Washington for a Caribbean cruise aboard the *U.S.S. Tuscaloosa*. Weary from the months of crisis touched off by the fall of France and the rigors of the recent presidential campaign, Roosevelt, accompanied only by his personal staff and his close adviser, Harry L. Hopkins, looked forward to two weeks of relaxation in the warm, tropical sun. The war in Europe had entered another lull, and there seemed to be no immediate danger. The British had survived their greatest test; in August and September the R.A.F. had turned back the German aerial assault, and though massive night raids continued on British cities, the threat of invasion had passed. Italian advances in the desert of North Africa in the early fall had been checked, and General Sir Archibald Wavell was preparing a vigorous counterattack in Egypt. On the continent, Mussolini had invaded Greece in October only to meet with humiliating defeat. The powerful German armies were engaged in occupying the newly conquered regions of Western Europe, and for the time being at least, Hitler held them in leash.

As the *Tuscaloosa* moved leisurely across the Caribbean, Roosevelt casually inspected the American bases in the West Indies and entertained British colonial officials and their wives. During the days at sea the President fished, though with little success; at night there were long poker games. At prearranged points along the way Navy seaplanes delivered the White House mail and the various State papers requiring the President's signature. For a few hours the President's staff worked on the routine matters, Roosevelt examined the important dispatches, and then the whole party resumed its relaxed holiday mood.

On the morning of December 9 a Navy seaplane delivered a long personal letter from Winston Churchill. In 4000 words he described the grave course of the war, emphasizing Britain's critical need for American supplies. He pointed out that German submarines were taking a heavy toll of shipping. And he informed the President that Britain was running out of money. By June England would exhaust her financial reserves and would no longer be able to pay for goods ordered from the United States. Promising that Britain would "suffer and sacrifice to the utmost for the Cause," Churchill expressed his confidence that the President would find the "ways and means" to continue furnishing England the material aid necessary to win the war.[1]

For another week Roosevelt continued his vacation while he considered this new problem. He was gay and carefree, but reticent with his companions. High governmental officials in Washington learned of Churchill's plea and waited anxiously for Roosevelt's return. On December 16 the President arrived in Washington, tanned and rested. The next day, at his press conference, he revealed his bold and imaginative response to Britain's financial crisis. He began by telling the reporters that he was convinced England was America's first line of defense. Since Britain needed supplies to help protect American security, the simplest solution, the President suggested, would be to lease the materials. "Now, what I am trying to do," Roosevelt said, "is eliminate the dollar sign."[2] Then in an apt parable, he compared his idea to lending a garden hose to a neighbor whose house was on fire. You didn't sell your hose to the neighbor, you loaned it to him, and he gave it back when the fire was out. So it would be with the munitions Britain needed to defeat Hitler.

The concept of lend-lease, first stated in these homey words, was Roosevelt's reply to Churchill's plea. The popular response was overwhelmingly favorable, and Roosevelt elaborated on

[1]*Foreign Relations, 1940*, III, 25.
[2]Robert Sherwood, *Roosevelt and Hopkins* (New York, 1948), p. 225.

the idea in a fireside chat to the American people on the evening of December 29. Again he stressed the importance of England to American security. "If Great Britain goes down, the Axis powers will control the continents of Europe, Asia, Africa, Australia, and the high seas," Roosevelt warned. "It is no exaggeration to say that all of us in the Americas would be living at the point of a gun. . . . " The President reiterated his campaign pledge to keep the nation out of the war, and he contended that increased aid to England was the best means available to insure against American involvement. "Emphatically we must get these weapons to them in sufficient volume and quickly enough, so that we and our children will be saved the agony and suffering of war which others have had to endure. . . . We must be," the President concluded, "the great arsenal of democracy."[3]

In early January, Treasury Department lawyers translated Roosevelt's formula into appropriate legislation. The basic authority they would seek for the President was simple—the power "to sell, transfer title to, exchange, lease, lend, or otherwise dispose of" any defense article to "the government of any country whose defense the President deems vital to the defense of the United States."[4] This lend-lease bill, shrewdly numbered H.R. 1776, was introduced into Congress on January 10. At committee hearings in both Houses administration spokesmen repeated the arguments that Roosevelt had made and revealed with embarrassing clarity the financial plight of Great Britain. Isolationists, led by Charles A. Lindbergh, appealed to Congressmen and Senators to defeat legislation which could lead only to American entry in the war. Let us "preserve one stronghold of order and sanity even against the gates of hell," pleaded historian Charles A. Beard.[5] But the isolationists were in the minority. Americans from every walk of life and every shade of political opinion announced their support for the President's policy. When Wendell Willkie,

[3]State Department, *Peace and War: United States Foreign Policy, 1931–1941* (Washington, 1943), pp. 601, 605, 607.
[4]*Ibid*, p. 628.
[5]William L. Langer and S. Everett Gleason, *The Undeclared War, 1940–1941* (New York, 1953), p. 278.

titular leader of the Republican party, endorsed lend-lease in mid-February, he made it a bipartisan issue, and thus guaranteed favorable action by Congress.

After brief and responsible debate the House passed the lend-lease bill by a margin of 260 to 161. In the Senate a small band of opponents, led by Democrat Burton Wheeler of Montana and Republican Gerald Nye of North Dakota, spent more than two weeks denouncing both Franklin Roosevelt and Great Britain, but to no avail. The Senate passed the lend-lease bill by a vote of 60-31, and on March 11 the President signed the new act. Within the next month Congress appropriated $7 billion to insure the continued flow of supplies to Britain and her allies in the war against the Axis.

The enactment of lend-lease was a major turning point in American foreign policy. Congress approved the decision to render all-out aid to Britain, reached by the administration during the dark days of the German blitzkrieg in the spring of 1940. The overwhelming margins indicated that the nation was now firmly committed to the goal of defeating Hitler. The great majority of the American people still hoped to achieve this objective by peaceful means. Yet by giving Britain unrestricted access to America's industrial resources, the United States took a major step toward war.

I

While Congress deliberated over the lend-lease proposals, an equally significant discussion was taking place secretly in Washington. From January 29 until March 27 representatives of the British Chiefs of Staff met with their American counterparts to coordinate military strategy in the event the United States entered the war against Germany. These talks stemmed from a memorandum submitted by Admiral Harold R. Stark, the Chief of Naval Operations, to President Roosevelt on November 12, 1940. Worried over the lack of planning for national defense, Stark sketched out the alternatives confronting the United States and stated his belief that "the continued existence of the British Empire" was crucial for the defense of the

Western Hemisphere. "I also believe," Stark continued, "that Great Britain requires from us very great help in the Atlantic, and possibly even on the continents of Europe and of Africa, if she is to be enabled to survive."[6] Therefore, Stark recommended that if the United States should become involved in war against the three Axis powers, it should concentrate its efforts in the Atlantic against Germany and stand on the defensive toward Japan in the Pacific. Finally, to prepare for such a situation, Stark asked the President for permission to hold staff conversations with the British military and naval leaders.

With characteristic caution, the President refused to sanction Stark's Atlantic policy, but he did permit the staff meetings to take place. In mid-January the British battleship *King George V* brought Lord Halifax, the new ambassador, to Washington; also on board were five senior English officers dressed in civilian clothes and listed as "technical advisers" to the British Purchasing Commission. For the next two months they met with American military and naval leaders to draw up plans for joint strategy in case of American involvement in the war. They quickly ratified the fundamental decision made by Stark in November: in a war with Germany and Japan, the United States and Britain would concentrate on defeating Germany first. Other points provoked disagreement, but the staff talks ended on March 27 with the adoption of a joint plan, "ABC-1," which the two nations would follow if the United States entered the war. This military coordination, together with the passage of lend-lease, signified that the United States, while still technically a neutral, had entered into what Robert Sherwood so aptly termed a "common law alliance" with Great Britain.

The adoption of ABC-1 provided for future cooperation between the United States and Great Britain, but the immediate problem facing the two nations in the winter and spring of 1941 was the renewed German submarine onslaught. When Hitler was compelled to give up his plans to invade Britain in the fall of 1940, he adopted the advice of Admiral Erich Raeder, Commander in Chief of the German Navy, and began

[6]*Ibid.*, p. 222.

an intensive campaign to sever England's supply lines to the United States and the Empire. German submarines, now operating out of bases on the French coast near the Atlantic sea lanes, developed new wolfpack techniques to penetrate British convoys and take an ever-heavier toll of merchant shipping. Groups of from eight to ten submarines would patrol together, and once a convoy was sighted, they would wait until nightfall to make a surface attack, thereby eluding the sensitive sonar gear aboard the British escort vessels. The German commanders submerged after firing the torpedoes, and would surface again to renew the attack. These tactics were strikingly successful; British shipping losses rose from 320,048 tons in January to 653,960 in April. "The situation is obviously critical in the Atlantic," wrote Admiral Stark on April 4. "In my opinion, it is hopeless except as we take strong measures to save it."[7]

Throughout the lend-lease debate American naval leaders wrestled with the problem of overcoming the German submarine attacks and insuring the safe delivery of supplies to Britain. On February 1 Admiral Stark directed that the naval units engaged in patrolling the hemisphere neutrality belt in the Atlantic be designated as the Atlantic Fleet. Two weeks later he ordered the commander of the new fleet, Rear Admiral Ernest J. King, to create a Support Force which would take over the task of escorting transatlantic convoys from the overburdened British Navy. For the next few weeks, 27 destroyers, four squadrons of Catalina patrol planes, and a number of minesweepers and tenders underwent intensive training in antisubmarine warfare. On March 20 the Navy informed President Roosevelt that it was now prepared to undertake convoy duty in the North Atlantic.

The Navy's statement presented the President with a critical political decision. During the lend-lease debate the administration had barely been able to avoid an amendment prohibiting the use of American naval vessels in convoying supplies to Britain. When the Committee to Defend America by Aiding the Allies started calling for such convoys in mid-March, isola-

[7]Samuel Eliot Morison, *The Battle of the Atlantic* (Boston, 1947), p. 56.

tionists in the press and Congress made a loud outcry. Senator Burton K. Wheeler of Montana declared that he realized that as soon as lend-lease was enacted, "the warmongers in this country would cry for convoys, and everyone recognizes the fact that convoys mean war."[8] On March 31 Senator Charles W. Tobey of New Hampshire introduced an anticonvoy resolution in Congress which touched off a long debate. At the same time public opinion polls revealed that a majority of the American people opposed employing the United States Navy to insure delivery of war materials to Britain.

The President hesitated to act in the face of such strong public resistance, but members of his administration warned that without American convoys, the lend-lease supplies would never reach Britain. On March 24 Secretary of the Navy Frank Knox and Secretary of War Henry L. Stimson agreed that convoying was "the only solution."[9] The next day Adolf Hitler intensified the problem by extending the war zone in which he permitted his submarines commanders to operate several hundred miles westward to include the waters adjacent to Greenland. For the next two weeks the President studied the problem, torn between a desire to aid Britain and fear of public disapproval.

On April 2, urged on by Stimson and Knox, Roosevelt approved Hemisphere Defense Plan No. 1, which authorized the Navy to undertake aggressive action against German submarines in the Western Atlantic. The question of convoys still had to be faced, and at a White House meeting on April 10 attended by Harry Hopkins and four cabinet members, including Stimson and Knox, the President compromised. Announcing that Congressional hostility precluded the use of the American Navy for convoys, Roosevelt said that instead he would authorize the extension of naval patrols beyond the 300-mile neutrality belt out into the mid-Atlantic. Secretary Stimson recorded the decision in his diary:

We had the atlas out and by drawing a line midway between the westernmost bulge of Africa and the easternmost bulge of Brazil, we

---

[8]Langer and Gleason, *Undeclared War*, p. 443.
[9]Henry L. Stimson and McGeorge Bundy, *On Active Service in Peace and War* (New York, 1948), p. 367.

found that the median line between the two continents was at about longitude line 25. . . . His plan is then that we shall patrol the high seas west of this median line, . . . and follow the [British] convoys and notify them of any German raiders or German submarines that we may see and give them a chance to escape.[10]

In effect, Roosevelt decreed that the Western Hemisphere began halfway across the Atlantic at longitude 25°. American naval units would patrol this area, but their precise mission remained undefined. Roosevelt did not make his new policy public, but later the same day the White House announced that on April 9 the United States government had signed an executive agreement with the Danish minister in exile placing Greenland under the protection of the United States and authorizing the construction of American air and naval bases there. The President justified this bold step, taken to prevent Germany from using Greenland as a supply depot for its submarines, as a measure for the defense of the Western Hemisphere. The next day Roosevelt sent a cable to Winston Churchill notifying him of the new patrol zone in the Atlantic and stating that the American Navy would inform the British of the presence of "aggressor ships or planes" that ventured into this area.[11]

The decision to occupy Greenland and to patrol the western half of the Atlantic completed Roosevelt's response to the Battle of the Atlantic in the spring of 1941. His advisers, especially Stimson and Knox, continued to press for convoys, but at a White House meeting on April 15 the President ruled out this alternative by rescinding Hemisphere Defense Plan No. 1, which sanctioned aggressive action against German submarines in the patrol zone and would have made convoying permissible. In its place, Roosevelt ordered Admiral Stark to limit naval activity in the Atlantic to intensive patrols. The President specifically stated that American ships were not to shoot at German submarines. Under these limitations it would be impossible for the Navy to provide escorts for British convoys. This compromise policy failed to provide England with all the help she needed to bring lend-lease supplies across the Atlantic

[10]*Ibid*, p. 368.
[11]Langer and Gleason, *Undeclared War*, p. 435.

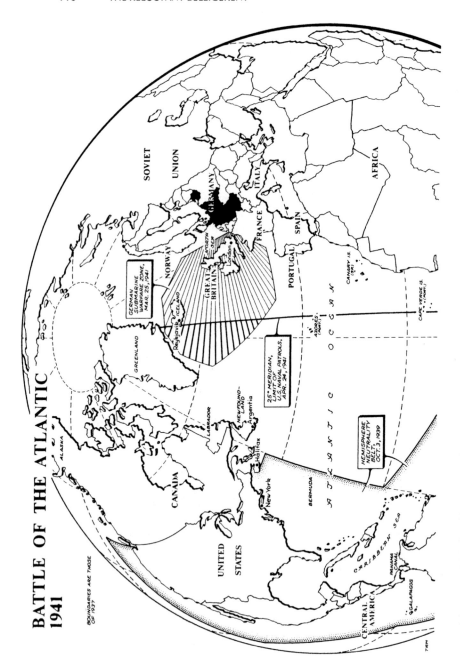

BATTLE OF THE ATLANTIC
1941

BOUNDARIES ARE THOSE
OF 1937

ALASKA

CANADA

UNITED
STATES

GREENLAND

LABRADOR

NEWFOUND-
LAND

Argentia

Halifax

New York

CENTRAL
AMERICA

GALAPAGOS
IS.

PANAMA
CANAL

CARIBBEAN SEA

BERMUDA

A T L A N T I C   O C E A N

HEMISPHERE
NEUTRALITY
BELT,
OCT. 3, 1939

25° MERIDIAN,
LIMIT OF
U.S. NAVAL PATROLS,
APR. 24, 1941

GERMAN
SUBMARINE
WARFARE ZONE,
MAR. 25, 1941

Reykjavik

ICELAND

NORWAY

GREAT
BRITAIN

London

NORTH
SEA

GERMANY

FRANCE

ITALY

SPAIN

PORTUGAL

AZORES
(PORT.)

CANARY IS.
(SP.)

CAPE VERDE IS.
(PORT.)

AFRICA

SOVIET

UNION

safely, but it did quiet the uproar in Congress. On April 30 the Senate Foreign Relations Committee tabled the Tobey anti-convoy resolution. The isolationists had been unable to enact a legislative restriction on American foreign policy, but they had succeeded in preventing Roosevelt from using American ships to convoy supplies to Britain.

Meanwhile, spring brought to the continent of Europe another massive German offensive. Striking from bases in Bulgaria, Hitler's forces moved swiftly throughout Yugoslavia and Greece despite fierce resistance in this mountainous terrain. The British rushed troops into northern Greece, but these reinforcements failed to stop the German panzer divisions. By the end of April, Hitler was master of the Balkans, and the British had been compelled to withdraw their forces to the island of Crete. And even here, protected by a broad stretch of open water, they were not safe. In early June Germany launched a parachute assault that caught the British on Crete by surprise and led to humiliating defeat. These reverses in Greece and Crete in turn weakened the British position in North Africa. During the winter General Wavell had routed the Italian armies in Libya, but in April General Rommel took advantage of the diversion of British forces to the Balkans to deliver a counterattack that drove the English back into Egypt. For the British, cheered by the successful defense of their home island in the fall, spring had brought a series of defeats that made ultimate victory in the war appear hopeless.

In the Atlantic, despite the new American patrol, the outlook was equally gloomy. Hitler's naval leaders had discovered a gap in the British convoy system—escort vessels based in Canada left the eastbound convoys in mid-Atlantic—and the merchant ships were easy targets until they were met by naval units from England. In April and May German wolfpacks converged on this vulnerable zone south of Iceland and took a heavy toll of British shipping. Then on May 24 disaster struck. The German battleship *Bismarck*, accompanied by the cruiser *Prinz Eugen*, slipped out of its base in Norway and headed for the open Atlantic. A British naval squadron moved to intercept the German ships, but in a brief encounter between Iceland and Greenland the *Bismarck* sank the British battle cruiser *Hood*, damaged the battleship *Prince of Wales*, and sailed south toward the convoy routes. Until the British Navy could intercept the *Bismarck* and destroy it, all shipping in the North Atlantic was imperiled. Two days later a British patrol plane finally located the German ships, and on May 27 units of the British Navy sank the *Bismarck*.

That same evening President Roosevelt spoke to the nation over the radio. His speech, the first major policy address in five months, had been postponed because of illness, and public interest in the President's words, heightened by the dramatic events on the high seas, was intense. Eighty-five million people heard him review the course of the war in Europe and point out the dangers German victory posed for the United States. Focusing on the Battle of the Atlantic, Roosevelt warned that Nazi success on the sea "would jeopardize the immediate safety of portions of North and South America." Announcing that naval patrols were already helping to protect the flow of goods to England, he bluntly declared, "The delivery of supplies to Britain is imperative. This can be done; it must be done; it will be done." Roosevelt then concluded his address by proclaiming a state of "unlimited national emergency."[12]

The President's speech evoked an enthusiastic response from the American people, but many thoughtful observers were puzzled over his failure to discuss the convoy issue. At a press conference the next day reporters asked the President if his determination to use all possible measures to deliver supplies to Britain meant that he planned to have the Navy begin convoying. To the dismay of interventionists, Roosevelt said no, indicating in a vague way that naval escorts were outmoded. He then astonished the press by commenting that he had no plans to issue the executive orders necessary to implement his declaration of an unlimited national emergency.

The speech of May 27, often hailed as a major turning point in American foreign policy, confirmed rather than altered the drift of Presidential policy. The passage of the Lend-Lease Act had raised the question of using American naval vessels to convoy supplies to Britain. Caught in a crossfire between isola-

---

[12]State Department, *Peace and War*, pp. 666, 669–70, 672.

tionists and internationalists, the President hesitated, realizing that if American destroyers accompanied British ships across the Atlantic, they were bound to become engaged in naval action with German submarines. He was convinced that the American people were not yet ready for such direct involvement in the European war.

II

The United States continued to grope for policies to contain Japanese aggression. After penetrating into northern Indo-China and signing the Tripartite Pact in the late summer of 1940, the Japanese had remained quiet. Their leaders waited for the outcome of the Battle of Britain, and when England succeeded in holding out against the German air attacks, Japan refrained from moving toward Malaya, Singapore, and Burma. The problem confronting American and British planners was to insure continued Japanese restraint. The basic military strategy suggested by Admiral Stark and embodied in ABC-1 gave priority to the war against Germany and outlined a defensive stance in the Far East. Diplomatically, this meant that the United States would have to find ways of blocking further Japanese expansion into Southeast Asia short of a military showdown. American diplomats thus faced the difficult task of devising a policy that fell between the equally dangerous extremes of appeasement and provocation.

One obvious way to divert the Japanese from moving into Southeast Asia would be to intensify their difficulties in China. As long as the Chinese could maintain effective resistance, an important part of the Japanese war machine would be tied down. In November 1940, when Chiang Kai-Shek appealed to the United States for military and financial support, President Roosevelt was highly receptive. On November 30 the White House announced that the United States would loan China $100 million. Privately, the administration promised Chiang fifty pursuit planes, and began considering a scheme, adopted in the spring, to allow Army, Navy, and Marine Corps aviators to resign their commissions and join Colonel Claire L. Chennault's "Flying Tigers," the American-manned nucleus of the Chinese Air Force. The desperate needs of a beleaguered Britain for American military supplies, coupled with the difficulty in delivering goods to China, prevented the United States from giving Chiang the massive aid he needed to drive the Japanese out of China, but the token assistance did keep China in the war, and thereby helped deter Japan from further aggression in Asia.

The Japanese dependence on the United States for supplies of oil, iron and steel, and other critical materials gave American planners a more direct means of influencing Japanese foreign policy. The ban on aviation gasoline in July and on all scrap iron and steel in September had marked the beginning of a policy of economic sanctions that moved steadily in the direction of a total embargo. In December 1940 iron ore, pig iron, and many forms of finished steel were added to the prohibited list. The following month the United States banned the export of copper and brass to Japan, and then almost weekly, additional materials came under the embargo. By the spring of 1941 Japanese industry was feeling a severe pinch from the shortage of critical supplies; in some cases, carefully hoarded stockpiles were exhausted and production of key items was impeded.

The most critical material of all, however, continued to flow uninterrupted to Japan. Except for the ban on aviation fuel, Japan was able to purchase all the petroleum that she could ship from the United States. Despite mounting pressure from Great Britain, Secretary of State Cordell Hull refused to consent to an embargo on oil. Hull feared that a policy of all-out economic pressure would lead to war, and he only agreed to the restrictions on lesser items to serve as a warning to Japan. The Secretary believed that Japan's dependence on the United States for oil was America's ultimate diplomatic weapon, and that it should not be used until all other means had failed and the nation was prepared to go to war. So long as the military plan called for a defensive stance in the Pacific, Hull preferred to seek accommodation with the Japanese.

The gradual American embargo worried the Japanese, and led them to seek a settlement with the United States in the early months of 1941. The first approach came informally, through two Catholic missionaries in Japan, Bishop James E. Walsh and Father James M. Drought. A prominent Japanese banker indicated to Walsh and Drought in December 1940 that some Japanese governmental leaders were concerned over the deteriorating relations with the United States and that they wished to seek a peaceful settlement. When Walsh and Drought returned to the United States in January 1941, they conferred with Postmaster General Frank C. Walker, a prominent Catholic, who arranged for them to meet with President Roosevelt. At the White House meeting, attended by Hull and Walker, the Catholic missionaries reported that the Japanese were willing to withdraw from the Tripartite Pact and remove their troops from China in return for a restoration of free trade with the United States. Although Hull and Roosevelt were dubious, they directed Drought and Walsh to "continue their contacts with the Japanese Embassy on a purely private basis and seek to reduce to writing what the Japanese had in mind."[13] The Japanese responded favorably to this suggestion, sending Colonel Hideo Iwakuro, a high official of the War Ministry, to meet with the Catholic missionaries and draw up a draft agreement.

While these informal negotiations were under way, Japan sent a new ambassador, Admiral Kichisaburo Nomura, to Washington in an effort to improve relations with the United States. Nomura, who had served briefly as Foreign Minister in 1939, was a retired naval officer who had many American friends and was known to be sympathetic to the United States. On February 14 President Roosevelt received Nomura officially at the White House, and in the course of their conversation, the President suggested that the ambassador meet informally with Cordell Hull from time to time to discuss the issues which separated their two countries. Three weeks later, on March 8, the first of some forty such meetings took place in the Secretary's Washington hotel suite. "There," writes Herbert Feis, "in the air, which like all hotel air, seems to belong to no one, they exchanged avowals of their countries' policies. And there,

[13]*The Memoirs of Cordell Hull* (2 vols.; New York, 1948), II, 985.

among furniture which, like all hotel furniture, is neutral, they sought formulas which would make them friends."[14] Despite the sincerity of both men, the obstacles were very great. Nomura came to persuade the United States to accede to the Japanese plans for a New Order in Asia; Hull was determined to convince the Japanese that expansion was wrong on moral grounds. Working without a translator, Nomura, whose English was halting, frequently misunderstood Hull, and even when he grasped the words, he failed to comprehend the moral principles which Hull insisted must be the basis of any settlement between the countries.

While Secretary Hull and Ambassador Nomura began their negotiations, the Catholic missionaries and Colonel Iwakuro drew up a draft agreement which they submitted to the State Department on April 9. Written by Iwakuro and translated into English by Father Drought, the document came as a severe disappointment to Hull. It contained no promise of Japanese withdrawal from China; instead, the Japanese asked that the United States cease its aid to China and influence Chiang to make peace on terms favorable to Japan. Nor did the agreement provide for Japanese withdrawal from the Tripartite Pact. The most Japan promised was to honor the alliance only if the United States attacked Germany. On the other major issue, the Japanese agreed not to engage in aggression in Southeast Asia provided that the United States remove its trade restrictions. The Secretary and his advisers found these terms unacceptable, but Hull decided not to reject the proposals outright, preferring to discuss them with Nomura in hopes of arriving at a more satisfactory settlement.

On April 14 Hull met with Nomura in his hotel suite and asked him if the Japanese government was submitting the draft agreement as a basis for negotiation. When Nomura replied that his government had not yet approved the text, Hull suggested that he refer it back to Tokyo. Two days later, Hull told Nomura that there were four basic principles Japan would have to accept as the basis of any settlement — respect for territorial integrity, noninterference in internal affairs of other

[14]Herbert Feis, *The Road to Pearl Harbor* (Princeton, 1950), p. 171.

countries, equality of commercial opportunity, and respect for the *status quo* in the Pacific. Very carefully and very precisely, Hull told Nomura that if the Japanese government would accept these four principles and would submit the draft proposals of April 9 as a basis of negotiation, the United States would offer counterproposals and a constructive settlement might be reached.

Unfortunately, Nomura misunderstood what Hull was saying. He notified his government that the United States had approved of the draft agreement of April 9 and asked the Japanese Foreign Office to give its consent. Nowhere did he mention the four basic principles Hull had laid down as a precondition to negotiation. Consequently, the Japanese leaders in Tokyo treated the draft agreement as an American plan and they prepared a counterproposal containing terms even more favorable to Japan. When Nomura delivered this reply to Hull in mid-May, the Secretary was astonished, and though he continued the negotiations, he realized that there was virtually no chance for a successful outcome. Nomura's inadequate knowledge of English and lack of skill as a diplomat had led to a tragic misunderstanding, which doomed a promising effort to heal the breach between the United States and Japan.

The stalemate in the Hull-Nomura conversations forced the Japanese to reassess the possibilities for expansion in Asia. The Army leaders, always the most militant group, favored a movement into southern Indo-China to acquire bases for a future assault on Malaya and the Dutch East Indies. In April Foreign Minister Yosuke Matsuoka had taken an important preparatory step by signing a neutrality treaty with the Soviet Union. In case either party became involved in war, the other agreed to remain neutral. Thus, if Japan moved into Southeast Asia and became involved in war with Britain and the United States, the northern flank would be secure. Yet two months later, to the astonishment of Matsuoka, the neutrality pact had an entirely different effect. On June 22, 1941, Hitler broke his nonaggression pact with Stalin and invaded the Soviet Union. Now Japan had to choose between two tempting courses of action. She could join with her German ally and attack Russia in Siberia, and thus remove for all time the threat from the north. Or Japan could take advantage of the German invasion of Russia to strike to the south, where the oil, rice, and mineral wealth of Thailand, Malaya, and the Indies lay exposed.

The Japanese reached their decision in a series of cabinet meetings in late June. Despite the entreaties of Hitler and the urging of Matsuoka, the cabinet decided not to move against Russia in the immediate future. Instead, Japan would demand that the Vichy French government grant her the right to station troops, build air fields, and occupy harbors in southern Indo-China, a move viewed as preparatory to the establishment of the Greater East Asia Co-Prosperity Sphere. This program was presented to the Emperor and formally adopted on July 2, 1941. In recording these decisions; the official record stated that in pursuing this policy, "we will not be deterred by the possibility of being involved in a war with England and America."[15] Japan had decided to move south and risk war with the United States rather than give in to the American economic pressure.

American diplomats learned of the crucial Japanese decision almost as soon as it was made. In the spring naval intelligence officers had cracked the Japanese diplomatic codes and were deciphering all dispatches from Tokyo to the embassy in Washington. This foreknowledge of Japanese policy, appropriately code-named "Magic," enabled American officials to consider what steps they might take to retaliate against the expected Japanese move into southern Indo-China. Secretary of the Treasury Henry Morgenthau had been advocating a total embargo since December, suggesting that this could be achieved by freezing all Japanese funds in the United States. In June Secretary of the Interior Harold Ickes, recently placed in charge of American petroleum policy, joined the British in calling for an oil embargo. Cordell Hull continued to oppose an embargo, but his frail health failed him in early July, and he was compelled to convalesce at White Sulphur Springs while the cabinet debated the issue of sanctions. The President, who would make the final decision, was uncertain. Pressed by Ickes to impose an oil embargo, he replied on July

[15]*Ibid*, p. 216.

JAPANESE
EXPANSION
1937-1941

SOVIET   UNION

OUTER
MONGOLIA

MANCHURIA

JEHOL

SAKHALIN

KARAFUTO

KURILES

NEPAL

Peking

KOREA

JAPANESE
EMPIRE

CHINA

Chungking

Nanking

Shanghai

YANGTZE

Tokyo

PACIFIC

MARCUS

BURMA
(BR.)

Canton

RYUKYUS

Hanoi

Hong Kong
(BR.)

FORMOSA

OCEAN

INDIA
(BR.)

THAI-
LAND

FRENCH
INDO-CHINA

HAINAN

MARIANAS

Saigon

Manila

ISLANDS

EQUATOR

MALAY
STATES
(BR.)

SPRATLEY

PHILIPPINE
ISLANDS
(U.S.)

GUAM
(U.S.)

INCLUDES
THE
MARSHALL
ISLANDS

Singapore

SARAWAK
(BR.)

SUMATRA

BORNEO

PALAU

CAROLINE   ISLANDS

INDIAN

NETHERLANDS

JAVA

CELEBES

OCEAN

EAST

CERAM

INDIES

NEW
GUINEA

AUSTRALIA

JAPAN AND AREAS
UNDER JAPANESE CONTROL
BEFORE THE INVASION
OF CHINA, JULY 7, 1937

JAPAN AND AREAS
UNDER JAPANESE CONTROL,
SUMMER, 1941

TRM

1, "I simply have not got enough Navy to go round—and every little episode in the Pacific means fewer ships in the Atlantic."[16] But news of the Japanese decision to move south convinced Roosevelt that the United States had to act. On July 10 Under Secretary of State Sumner Welles informed the British that the President had authorized him to state that if Japan took "any overt step" in Southeast Asia, the United States "would immediately impose various embargoes, both economic and financial. . . ."[17]

For the next two weeks the administration debated the nature of the embargoes. Secretary Hull sent frequent messages from White Sulphur Springs urging caution, and he found an ally in Admiral Stark. In a study of the effect of an embargo on Japanese-American relations, the War Plans Division of the Navy warned that Japan would respond by invading the Dutch East Indies to gain access to petroleum. Stark sent this memorandum to the President on July 21, adding that he concurred with its conclusions. But when it was learned that the Japanese had demanded bases from the French in southern Indo-China, and had warned that they would begin to occupy this region on July 24, the mood in Washington hardened. On July 23, Welles called Nomura to the State Department to inform him that Hull was breaking off their talks. The next day, after news was received that Japan had invaded southern Indo-China, the cabinet met and Roosevelt announced that he planned to impound all Japanese funds in the United States, thereby severing trade with Japan. At 8 P.M. on July 25 the White House announced that the President was freezing all Japanese assets, and the next day the necessary executive orders were issued.

The American people believed that the administration had finally decided on a total embargo on oil shipments to Japan. The press voiced strong support for such a move. "The noose is around Japan's neck at last," applauded an editorial writer in *PM*. "For a time it may bluster and retaliate, but in the end it can only whimper and capitulate."[18] But in fact the President

[16]Elliott Roosevelt, ed., *F.D.R.: His Personal Letters, 1928–1945* (2 vols.; New York, 1950), II, 1173–74.

[17]Feis, *Road to Pearl Harbor*, p. 227.

[18]Langer and Gleason, *Undeclared War*, p. 652.

had not intended to cut off all oil shipments. Instead he believed that the freezing order could be used to pressure Japan by giving the administration a new weapon to reduce and control the amount of petroleum exported to Japan. If the Japanese proved uncooperative, then the order could be used to achieve a total embargo. Thus on July 31 he approved new regulations to permit the release of blocked funds sufficient to enable Japan to purchase oil at prewar levels.[19]

The actual embargo was the result of bureaucratic initiative by Assistant Secretary of State Dean G. Acheson. In early August, Acheson used his position on the Foreign Funds Control Committee to frustrate Japanese attempts to acquire the necessary licenses to unblock currency and purchase limited amounts of oil. This de facto embargo was in effect for several weeks before Secretary of State Hull became aware of it. Given strong public approval for the cut-off and the realization that Japan would take any relaxation as a sign of weakness, Hull decided to sanction the embargo as official American policy on September 5.[20] The result was to confirm the decision for war that Japan had already reached. With only a year's supply of oil on hand, Japan was confronted with a clear-cut choice — either give up plans for the New Order or defy the United States by seizing the vital oil of the Dutch East Indies. Joseph Grew, the American ambassador in Tokyo, had no illusions about the consequences. "The obvious conclusion," he confided to his diary, "is eventual war."[21]

III

The German decision to invade Russia had a profound impact on the European war. For Great Britain, standing alone since the fall of France, the German drive to the east was a momentous turning point. Coming after British defeats in Greece, Crete, and North Africa, and at a time when the U-

[19]Irvine H. Anderson, Jr., *The Standard-Vacuum Oil Company and United States East Asian Policy, 1933–1941* (Princeton, 1975), pp. 174-76.

[20]Jonathan G. Utley, "Upstairs, Downstairs at Foggy Bottom: Oil Exports and Japan, 1940-41," *Prologue, VIII* (1976), 26-28.

[21]Langer and Gleason, *Undeclared War*, p. 654.

boat onslaught was at its height, Operation Barbarossa, as Hitler termed his Russian offensive, opened up the possibility of eventual victory over Germany through an Anglo-Soviet alliance. On the evening following the German attack, Churchill grimly embraced Stalin as a new ally in the war against Hitler. Recalling his long record of opposing Communism, the Prime Minister brushed aside the ideological issue. "Any man or state who fights on against Nazidom will have our aid," Churchill declared. "Any man or state who marches with Hitler is our foe." Then he added, "We shall appeal to our friends and allies in every part of the world to take the same course and pursue it, faithfully and steadfastly to the end. . . ."[22]

The American response to Russia's entry into the war was much more ambiguous. American diplomats in Europe had been warning for months that Germany was planning to attack Russia, but the actual invasion on June 22 caught American officials by surprise. Acting Secretary of State Sumner Welles hurriedly prepared a statement which he submitted to the President for approval and then released to the press on June 23. Echoing Churchill's remarks of the previous evening, Welles condemned "communistic dictatorship" but asserted that the issue was not the nature of the Soviet regime but the necessity of stopping Nazi plans for world conquest. "In the opinion of this Government, consequently, any defense against Hitlerism," Welles stated, ". . . will hasten the eventual downfall of the present German leaders, and will therefore redound to the benefit of our defense and security."[23] This statement, unlike Churchill's speech, failed to mention the question of aid to Russia, and thus left American policy unclear on this crucial point.

The next day Roosevelt spoke out a press conference more candidly. Asked to comment on the Welles statement, the President bluntly declared, "Of course we are going to give all aid we possibly can to Russia."[24] He then refused to specify whether such aid would come under lend-lease and proceeded

[22]Winston S. Churchill, *The Unrelenting Struggle* (New York, 1942), pp. 172-73.

[23]State Department, *Peace and War*, p. 684.

[24]Raymond H. Dawson, *The Decision to Aid Russia, 1941* (Chapel Hill, 1959), p. 121.

to dodge all queries about the amount and extent of assistance to the Soviets. Later the same day, June 24, the administration announced that some $40 million in Russian assets, which had been impounded along with German and Italian funds in the United States on June 14, had been released. Then the next day the White House announced that the President did not intend to invoke the Neutrality Act for the Russo-German war, thereby permitting American ships to carry supplies to the Pacific port of Vladivostok. These two announcements gave substance to the President's press conference remark: the $40 million and the use of American ships were essential for any program of aid to Russia.

The reaction of the American people to the German invasion of Russia was hesitant and confused. Isolationists tended to be jubilant when they learned of this new development. They were convinced that the United States would never fight side-by-side with Communists, and thus they felt that the chances of involvement in the European war had dropped sharply. Isolationist spokesmen quickly pointed out that instead of a war for democracy, the United States was confronted with "the death struggle between the armed might of Nazism and communism." "The question now is," asserted John T. Flynn, "are we going to fight to make Europe safe for Communism?" The answer, said Charles A. Lindbergh, is no. "I would a hundred times rather see my country ally herself with England, or even Germany with all her faults, than with the cruelty, the Godlessness, and the barbarism that exist in the Soviet Union," the aviator-hero told an America First rally.[25] Interventionists tended to be equally elated over the German move, but for very different reasons. They believed that Russia would drain off a great deal of Germany's strength, and thus give Britain a chance to build up her power and bring it to bear effectively. Few interventionist spokesmen advocated extending aid to Russia; instead they urged that the United States redouble its efforts to help Britain.

Public opinion tended to reflect only a reluctant sympathy for the Soviet Union. In polls taken in late June and early July, George Gallup found that over 70% of those questioned

[25]*Ibid.*, pp. 81, 82; Langer and Gleason, *Undeclared War*, p. 542.

NAZI ATTACK
ON RUSSIA, 1941

AXIS, ALLIES, OCCUPIED AREAS
AND FINLAND,
JUNE 21, 1941,

GERMAN GAINS
IN RUSSIA,
JUNE 22 TO DECEMBER, 1941

BOUNDARIES OF 1938

wanted to see Russia defeat Germany. But the ideological distrust of the Soviet Union still influenced many Americans. When asked if they favored the sending of war materials to Russia on the same basis that they were supplied to Britain, only 35% answered yes. Moreover, most Americans and almost all military experts did not believe that the Russians could survive the German invasion. The rapid Nazi advance and the memories of Russian ineptitude in the Winter War with Finland led both isolationists and interventionists to conclude that it was only a matter of months, perhaps even weeks, before Hitler would be the master of the Soviet Union. With Russia facing what appeared to be nearly certain defeat, it was, therefore, difficult to believe that Communism was a threat to American security. "Soviet ideology was hated, but Soviet power was not feared," comments Raymond Dawson.[26] It was this fact, more than any other, which led the American people to sympathize with the cause of Soviet resistance.

The Roosevelt administration, sharing the widespread doubt of Russia's ability to survive, did not launch any immediate program to assist the Soviet Union. Instead, Roosevelt's advisers urged taking advantage of the breathing space to increase its aid to Britain. Secretary of War Stimson reported on June 23 that Army leaders believed that Germany would defeat Russia in less than three months and that the United States should use "this precious and unforeseen period of respite" to develop a more vigorous policy in the Atlantic. Secretary of the Navy Frank Knox and Admiral Stark echoed this recommendation in messages to Roosevelt asking him to strike hard at Hitler while he was preoccupied with what they were certain would be a brief Russian campaign. In an interview with the President in late June, Admiral Stark urged Roosevelt to "seize the psychological opportunity presented by the Russian-German clash" and begin convoying British ships across the Atlantic.[27]

Roosevelt was impressed by this advice, and considered ways of extending further aid to Britain in the Atlantic. Even before

[26]Dawson, *Decision to Aid Russia*, p. 101.
[27]Sherwood, *Roosevelt and Hopkins*, p. 304; Dawson, *Decision to Aid Russia*, p. 115.

the German invasion of Russia, the President had approved plans to land American troops in Iceland and take over from Britain the job of protecting this key island from potential German aggression. Roosevelt insisted that this occupation must have the consent of the Icelandic government, and several snags developed before an invitation was issued by the Prime Minister of Iceland. On July 1 the United States reached an agreement, and a force of 4000 American marines set out for Iceland. The President then began preparation of a message to Congress announcing the new operation. He planned to justify this action on grounds of defending the Western Hemisphere, but many of his advisers, most notably Secretary Stimson, urged him to take a broader position. The nation should be told, urged Stimson, that the United States was taking control of Iceland to forestall German invasion, and that once in Iceland, the United States would use its position there to escort British convoys across the Atlantic.

The President was not yet willing to go so far. On June 30 Senator Burton K. Wheeler had introduced a resolution in Congress demanding that the Naval Affairs Committee investigate rumors that American ships were already escorting British convoys. Worried by this Congressional sniping, and aware that recent public opinion polls revealed that the American people were still evenly divided on the convoy issue, Roosevelt refused to sanction convoys. In his message to Congress on July 7 he justified the sending of troops to Iceland on the need to forestall German occupation, which would give Hitler bases "for eventual attack against the Western Hemisphere."[28] The President added that German seizure of Iceland would endanger all shipping in the Atlantic and interrupt the flow of supplies to Britain, but he did not announce any additional steps to protect the Atlantic supply line.

Although a few commentators criticized Roosevelt for straining the limits of the Western Hemisphere to include Iceland, the public response to the President's message was very favorable. Roosevelt was so encouraged that he decided to begin using American naval units for limited convoy duty in the Atlantic. On July 11 he approved Hemisphere defense

---

[28]State Department, *Peace and War*, p. 686.

Plan IV, which provided for "escort convoys of United States and Iceland flag shipping, including shipping of any nationality which may join such convoys, between the United States ports and bases, and Iceland."[29] By this rather devious means, British ships could join the relatively small number of Icelandic and American ships traveling between the United States and Iceland, and receive the protection of American Navy better than halfway across the Atlantic. Operations plans to this effect were issued on July 19, but before they went into effect on July 25 the President had changed his mind. Worried over the public reaction, at the last minute Roosevelt suspended the provision permitting "shipping of any nationality" to travel with American convoys. ". . . policy seems to be something never fixed, always fluid and changing," commented a disappointed Admiral Stark.[30] Once again, the President had drawn back from the momentous step of escorting British vessels across the hazardous waters of the North Atlantic. Despite repeated pleas from activists in his cabinet and polite promptings from Churchill, Roosevelt refused to make a move toward war with Germany which did not have the strong backing of the American people.

While Roosevelt undertook these limited steps to aid Britain in the Atlantic, the problem of aid to Russia became increasingly serious. In late June the Russian Ambassador in Washington called at the State Department and submitted a vast list of needed war materials, ranging from bombers and guns to rolling mills and machine tools. Sumner Welles, still serving as Acting Secretary while Hull recuperated at White Sulphur Springs, created a State Department committee on June 30 to approve and expedite Soviet orders. President Roosevelt was particularly impressed by the Russian request for factory supplies, which indicated they were preparing to fight a long war, and he was determined to supply as much aid as he possibly could. Influenced by reports from his ambassador in Moscow and the recommendations of the former American envoy there, Joseph Davies, Roosevelt ignored the advice of the

[29]Langer and Gleason, *Undeclared War*, p. 579.
[30]Patrick Abbazia, *Mr. Roosevelt's Navy: The Private War of The U.S. Atlantic Fleet, 1939–1942* (Annapolis, 1975), p. 216.

military experts and decided to gamble on the Soviet Union's surviving the German onslaught in the summer of 1941.

Without any public announcement the aid program for Russia got under way slowly in July. The overburdened State Department found it difficult to deal with problems of procurement and shipping, and in the middle of the month responsibility was shifted to the Division of Defense Aid Reports, which was the central clearing house for lend-lease. Under the direction of Colonel Philip R. Faymonville, a Russian-speaking army officer who had served as military attache in Moscow in the late 1930s, and who had a high regard for Soviet military capabilities, the aid program began to take form. But progress was slow; in July less than $7 million worth of supplies were sent to the Soviet Union. At a cabinet meeting on August 1 President Roosevelt lashed out as his subordinates, giving the State and War departments, according to Secretary of the Interior Ickes, "one of the most complete dressings down that I have witnessed." According to Henry Morgenthau, the President told his cabinet that "he didn't want to hear what was on order; he said he wanted to hear what was on the water."[31]

On August 2 the United States gave Russia its first formal commitment of assistance. In an exchange of notes with the Soviet Ambassador, Acting Secretary Welles promised to render "all economic assistance practicable for the purpose of strengthening the Soviet Union in its struggle against armed aggression." The note further stated that such aid was motivated by the belief that Soviet resistance to German aggression "is in the national interest of the United States."[32] This commitment was confirmed by the reports of Harry Hopkins, who flew to Moscow from England on July 30 and met with Stalin for several days to discuss Russian needs. Later in August Hopkins reported to Roosevelt his belief that Russia could hold out until the onset of winter.

On August 5 the State Department made public the exchange of notes with the Soviet Union announcing the

[31]*The Secret Diary of Harold L. Ickes* (3 vols.; New York, 1954), III, 592; Langer and Gleason, *Undeclared War*, p. 560.
[32]*Foreign Relations, 1941*, I, 815–16.

American aid program. The reaction of the American people was surprisingly favorable. In part, this was due to the increasingly effective resistance of the Red Army. After six weeks of war the German forces had penetrated over 150 miles into the Soviet Union, but they had failed to rout the Russian armies and the momentum of their drive was beginning to flag. For the first time since the start of the war, Germany had been unable to win a lightning victory in a land campaign. This was a heartening development for millions of Americans. Now perhaps Hitler could be defeated in Europe without the intervention of the United States. At the very least, the United States could give Russia the supplies she needed to continue her heroic resistance to Hitler. Always eager to believe that the nation's security could be protected short of entry into the European holocaust, Americans rallied behind the administration's decision to aid Russia.

Another major issue in the summer of 1941 revealed the continuing reluctance of the American people to contemplate entry into the war. The Selective Service Act, adopted in August 1940, contained two provisions which the administration found to be increasingly embarrassing. First, the act limited the time of service for all "selectees" to one year. The first men conscripted had entered the service in the fall of 1940 and were scheduled for release in the autumn of 1941 unless Congress changed the terms of the law. Second, Congress had insisted that men drafted into the army could not be stationed outside the Western Hemisphere. In June 1940 General George C. Marshall, Army Chief of Staff, asked the President for permission to have Congress remove these restrictions. Marshall warned that unless the term of service were extended, the new Army being created would melt away by the winter of 1942. Moreover, with the occupation of Iceland and the need to strengthen American forces in Hawaii and the Philippines, the Western Hemisphere limitation imposed severe handicaps on the Army.

President Roosevelt hesitated to press this issue, which was certain to stir up intense opposition in Congress, at a time when he was trying to unify the country behind his foreign policy. However, Secretaries Stimson and Knox strongly backed the suggested changes, and when Marshall provided a lucid and compelling statement of the need for change in his biennial report to the Secretary of War, Roosevelt agreed to risk the wrath of the isolationists in Congress. On July 10, the administration had three resolutions introduced in the Senate to amend the 1940 Selective Service Act. The resolutions would permit the President to keep draftees in service for the duration of the national emergency, would permit the sending of these men beyond the limits of the Western Hemisphere, and would remove the ceiling of 900,000 men imposed by Congress in 1940.

The opposition to these proposals was even greater than Roosevelt had expected. Many Congressmen who had loyally supported earlier administration foreign policy measures now balked. They charged that the extension of service constituted a breach of faith with the draftees, who had been promised a return to civilian life after 12 months duty. Moreover, many middle-of-the-road Congressmen feared giving the President the power to send the new Army overseas. Public opinion polls reflected the hostility of the American people. A clear majority opposed the removal of the Western Hemisphere restriction, while only a bare majority backed the extension of service. On July 14 Congressional leaders met with Roosevelt at the White House to report their belief that Congress would not accept these changes without modification. Accordingly, Roosevelt authorized his spokesmen in Congress to drop the request for permission to station draftees outside the Western Hemisphere and told the Congressional leaders to go all-out for extension of the time of service. In a radio address on July 21 the President issued a strong plea for public support, warning that in the midst of a grave national crisis "Americans cannot afford to speculate with the security of America."[33]

Debate on the Selective Service proposals began in the Senate on July 30. Led by the Senator Robert A. Taft of Ohio, a large group of Senators objected strenuously to the indefinite extension of the time of service. Although administration leaders were able to defeat Taft's amendment to limit exten-

[33]Samuel Rosenman, ed., *The Public Papers and Addresses of Franklin D. Roosevelt* (13 vols.; New York, 1938-1950, X, 275.

sion to six months, they finally were compelled to compromise and accept an amendment setting the additional length of service for draftees at eighteen months. On this basis the Senate passed the bill on August 7 by a vote of 45 to 30. The debate was even more explosive in the House. The leaders accepted the 18-month limitation, but even then opponents denounced the bill in scathing terms. The House acted on August 12, passing the measure by the incredible margin of one vote, 203 to 202.

The closeness of the vote mirrored the uncertainty of the public mood in the summer of 1941. Partisan politics of course influenced the final outcome. Many Republicans, and some Democrats, who favored the passage of the bill voted against it to win favor with their constituents back home, believing all the time that there were ample votes to pass the measure. But fundamentally the close ballot indicated that the American people were not convinced that Germany and Japan truly endangered the security of the United States. The near-panic which followed the fall of France had subsided, and after the German invasion of Russia, many Americans felt that the immediate danger of a German thrust into the Western Hemisphere had passed. Unconcerned by the effect of economic sanctions on Japan and hoping for a bloody statemate between the Nazi and Communist forces in Europe, the American people showed an amazing complacency in very nearly permitting what Marshall termed "the disintegration of the Army."[34]

IV

While Congress debated the future of American military preparedness, President Roosevelt met secretly with Prime Minister Winston Churchill off the coast of Newfoundland. The two leaders had planned to meet in the spring to coordinate American and British policy at the highest level. After repeated delays the conference took place aboard the warships *Augusta* and *Prince of Wales* from August 9 to August 12.

[34]Sherwood, *Roosevelt and Hopkins*, p. 367.

Although the original intention was for a meeting confined to the two leaders, this Atlantic Conference was expanded to include both military and diplomatic officials.

The talks ranged over a broad area, including the problems of supplying Russia, the convoy issue in the North Atlantic, the Japanese threat in Southeast Asia, and the outline of a postwar world order. Churchill and Roosevelt agreed on the necessity of giving Russia all possible aid to withstand the German attack, and the two leaders sent a message to Stalin proposing a conference of high-level representatives in Moscow in October to work out a long term program of supply. In the course of the naval staff conservations, the American and British representatives agreed that the United States should begin escorting convoys halfway across the Atlantic, and final arrangements for this procedure were formulated. However, the actual use of American naval units for convoy duty required Presidential approval, which was not yet forthcoming.

Roosevelt and Churchill concentrated on discussing the crisis in the Far East resulting from the Japanese movement into southern Indo-China and the subsequent freezing order of July 26. The British were very worried that Japan would respond by striking south through Malaya to the Dutch East Indies. In late July 1941 the Australian government had asked the British to secure a pledge from the United States to come to its aid if the Japanese moved south. In a conversation with the British Under Secretary of State for Foreign Affairs, Sir Alexander Cadogan, on the opening day of the conference, Sumner Welles pointed out that it would be very difficult for the President to make such a commitment. Welles urged instead that Britain and the United States pursue a policy of delay, dragging out conversations with the Japanese as long as possible, "in order to put off a show-down (if such was inevitable) until the time that such a show-down was from our standpoint more propitious."[35]

The British were not satisfied with this tactic. On August 10 Cadogan handed Welles the draft of parallel notes of warning to be sent to Japan by the United States, Great Britain, and the Netherlands. The notes stated that in the case of further

[35]*Foreign Relations, 1941*, I, 347.

Japanese aggression in Southeast Asia, each government "would be compelled to take counter measures even though these might lead to war." In a private conversation Churchill told Welles that in his opinion such warning notes to Japan were "in the highest degree important," and that unless the United States made such a clear-cut declaration to Japan, war was inevitable in Southeast Asia. The next day, August 11, Churchill pressed these arguments in a conference with Roosevelt. The President indicated that he preferred to continue discussing the outstanding issues with Japan, but he agreed to inform Nomura that if Japan undertook further aggression in Asia, America would respond with measures which "might result in war between the United States and Japan."[36] Churchill preferred a joint warning sent by the three powers simultaneously, but he agreed to the President's suggestion.

The conversations on the Far East at the Atlantic Conference disappointed the British. Hoping for a firm American commitment to deter Japan from futher expansion, they received only the promise of a unilateral American warning. When Roosevelt returned to Washington, Cordell Hull carefully watered down the proposed statement to Ambassador Nomura. Thus when Nomura called on Roosevelt at the White House on August 17, the President told him that if Japan moved toward the south, he would be compelled to take steps "toward insuring the safety and security of the United States."[37] This mild and ambiguous statement was a long way from Churchill's plea for a warning that the United States take measures that "might lead to war." Roosevelt was not duped by Churchill at the Atlantic Conference, as his critics charged; rather, the Presidents had skillfully evaded the Prime Minister's determined effort to commit the United States to a firm and unyielding stand against Japan.

The final subject discussed at the conference—the kind of postwar world the United States and Britain envisioned—led to the formation of the Atlantic Charter. The United States was primarily responsible for this declaration of principles. Roosevelt was concerned over the possibility that Britain and

[36]*Ibid.*, pp. 354, 355, 358.
[37]*Foreign Relations: Japan, 1931–1941*, II, 557.

Russia would make a deal concerning the territorial boundaries of postwar Europe. Secretary Hull and his aides in the State Department were equally upset over indications that Britain objected to American ideas for freer international trade in the postwar world. The American people feared that in joining with the Soviet Union, Britain might abandon the democratic ideals which Americans felt should undergird the crusade against Hitler. To alleviate these anxieties, the President suggested that he and Churchill release a statement of principle to the world.

Churchill was delighted with Roosevelt's suggestion. Unable to secure any commitments from the United States to enter the war, at least he could bind the United States to Britain's cause through a joint declaration of purpose. The British delegation submitted a five-point draft statement which became the basis for the Charter. The first three points stated unimpeachable principles—a pledge against aggression, a promise of self-determination in territorial changes, and respect for the right of self-government including freedom of speech. The fourth point dealt very vaguely with a liberal economic policy, while the fifth stated the determination of the two leaders to seek lasting peace by creating an "effective international organization."[38] Roosevelt and Welles accepted the first three points, but the last two underwent considerable change. The United States insisted on a more specific pledge for liberal international trade policies after the war. After lengthy debate the fourth point was broadened into two separate statements, points four and five in the Charter, which went part way toward satisfying the American position.

On the question of future world order, Roosevelt objected to the reference to international organization. He told Churchill that he could not agree to such a specific pledge "because of the suspicions and opposition that such a statement on his part would create in the United States." Indeed, Roosevelt continued, he felt that after the war a joint Anglo-American police force rather than a new League of Nations would be needed to preserve world peace. After much discussion the two leaders agreed on three points on the nature of the peace, including a pledge for freedom of the seas and the disarmament of aggressor nations "pending the establishment of a wider and permanent system of general security."[39] On August 14 the eight-point Atlantic Charter was announced to the world in the form of a press release. Isolationists raised an outcry at such close cooperation with a belligerent power, and charged that Roosevelt had signed secret commitments, but the majority of the American people responded enthusiastically to the principles of the Atlantic Charter.

If isolationists could have heard Winston Churchill report to his war cabinet on the Atlantic meeting, they would have had their worst fears confirmed. Churchill told his colleagues that FDR was determined to enter the war but had to act cautiously since "clearly he was skating on pretty thin ice in his relations with Congress." "The President had said that he would wage war but not declare it," Churchill continued, "and that he would become more and more provocative. . . . he would look for an 'incident' which would justify him in opening hostilities."[40] It is difficult to know how accurately Churchill was reporting on what Roosevelt told him at the Atlantic Conference — the President was very skillful at suggesting his agreement in a conversation without making any firm commitments. Unable to give Churchill the decision on convoying or the warning to Japan that the Prime Minister wanted, FDR evidently tried to reassure him of ultimate American entry into the conflict. Yet the closeness of the vote on Selective Service extension reinforced his natural caution and made him move carefully in extending aid to Britain and Russia. Roosevelt had led the nation to the brink of war by the summer of 1941 but he refused to take the final step until the nation was ready.

[39]*Ibid.*, pp. 363, 368-69.
[40]Joseph P. Lash, *Roosevelt and Churchill, 1939-1941: The Partnership That Saved the West* (New York, 1976), pp. 401-02.

CHAPTER VI

Accepting the Challenge

I N SEPTEMBER 1941 the Second World War entered its third year. The Axis powers were triumphant on all fronts. Germany controlled the major centers of population and industry in Europe. Her armies were moving deep within the Soviet Union, threatening Leningrad and Moscow and overrunning the fertile Ukraine and the industrial Donetz basin in the south. Stiffening Russian resistance denied Hitler the quick victory he confidently expected, but it appeared likely that he would complete his conquest of Russia by the spring of 1942. German submarines continued to take a heavy toll of English shipping in the North Atlantic, and Axis air power, striking from bases in Italy and Tunisia, closed the Mediterranean to the British, compelling them to supply their hard-pressed forces in Egypt by sending convoys around the Cape of Good Hope and up to the Red Sea. In the Far East, where Japan had been waging war since 1937, the outlook was no better. Japan controlled the entire coast of China and all her major cities. The occupation of Indo-China, completed in July, placed Japanese troops in a position to sweep over Southeast Asia and down into the Dutch East Indies. In this precarious world situation, America held the balance of power. If the United States continued to cling to its neutrality, the emergence of a New Order in Europe and Asia seemed assured.

The Roosevelt administration, aware of the importance of its decision on the course of the war, hardened its policy toward Japan in the early fall of 1941. Secretary Hull's decision on September 5 to accept Acheson's de facto oil embargo as official American policy proved to be the decisive step. Great Britain and Holland, puzzled at first by the ambiguous nature of the July 26 freezing order, cooperated by impounding Japanese assets and stopping all further shipments of petroleum to Japan. The last cargo of crude oil left the Dutch East Indies on August 5; after that, Japan was cut off from its traditional source of supply. The embargo quickly became a crucial factor for the policy makers in Tokyo. Although Japan had carefully stockpiled petroleum products throughout the 1930s, by 1941 she had only 18 months supply on hand. Oil was essential for the Japanese war effort; without gasoline the planes, tanks, and warships were useless. Japanese leaders each day witnessed the consumption of another 12,000 tons of petroleum. Either they must give in to the United States and abandon their ambitious plans of conquest, or they would have to stand and fight while they had the oil to do so. The endless round of negotiations between the two countries could no longer continue. "From now on the oil gauge and the clock stood side by side," commented Herbert Feis. "Each fall in the level brought the hour of decision closer."[1]

The Japanese Prime Minister, Prince Fumimaro Konoye, decided to undertake a bold step to break the deadlock. Realizing that Army and Navy leaders would insist on war rather than face surrender, Konoye proposed a personal meeting with President Roosevelt to seek a peaceful solution to the Japanese-American crisis. In Tokyo Konoye won the grudging consent of the military to pursue this plan, but only with the understanding that if Roosevelt refused to accept Japanese dominance in Asia, the Prime Minister would "be prepared to assume leadership in the war against America."[2] On August 8 Ambassador Nomura met with Cordell Hull, who had returned to Washington from White Sulphur Springs, to explore the issues separating their two countries. When Nomura suggested that the heads of government meet, possibly in Hawaii, Hull dismissed the proposal, stating that such a meeting would be impossible until Japan gave specific evidence of abandoning her aggressive policies in the Far East.

[1] *The Road to Pearl Harbor* (Princeton, 1950), p. 244. For the most recent discussion of American oil policy in 1941, see Irving H. Anderson, Jr., *The Standard-Vacuum Oil Company and United States East Asian Policy, 1933–1941* (Princeton, 1975), pp. 178–92.

[2] Feis, *Road to Pearl Harbor*, p. 253.

Undiscouraged, Nomura raised the idea again when he was called to the White House on August 17 to receive the warning that Roosevelt and Churchill had discussed at the Atlantic Conference. The President read two statements to the Japanese Ambassador, but they did not constitute the severe warning Churchill had wanted, and when the President had finished, Nomura again brought up the idea of a summit conference between Roosevelt and Konoye. The President was evidently intrigued with the idea, and although he made no commitment, he suggested that such a meeting might take place in Juneau, Alaska in mid-October.

The next day the Japanese Foreign Minister, Admiral Teijiro Toyoda, held a two-and-a-half hour conference with Ambassador Grew in Tokyo. Toyoda pleaded for a meeting between Roosevelt and Konoye, claiming that Japan did not want war, and that Konoye was breaking all precedent in proposing to leave his country to carry on negotiations. "This determination of Prince Konoye," Grew reported Toyoda as saying, "is nothing but the expression of his strongest desire to save the civilization of the world from ruin as well as to maintain peace in the Pacific by making every effort in his power. . . ." Toyoda's sincerity impressed Grew, and in a separate cable to the State Department, the Ambassador urged that the proposed meeting be given "very prayerful consideration." Grew felt it presented an opportunity to break through the "apparently insurmountable obstacles to peace" in the Far East.[3]

Worried by the lack of response from Washington, Prince Konoye a week later sent a personal message to the President. Reiterating his desire to avoid war between the United States and Japan, which he feared would lead to "the collapse of world civilization," Konoye stated his conviction that the poor relationship between the two countries was due to a serious lack of understanding that could be remedied only by an agreement between the heads of the two governments. In an accompanying document, submitted to Roosevelt by Nomura on August 28, the Konoye government gave its terms. Japan

[3]*Foreign Relations: Japan, 1931–1941*, II, 563, 565.

had occupied Indo-China in order to "accelerate the settlement of the China Incident" and intended to withdraw her forces as soon as the war in China could be ended. The note stated that Japan did not intend to use her position in Indo-China as a springboard to invade Southeast Asia. "In a word," the note pledged, "the Japanese Government has no intention of using, without provocation, military force against any neighboring nation."[4]

Cordell Hull did not believe the Japanese. Although President Roosevelt again indicated that he was receptive to the idea, Hull feared a trap and began to throw his considerable influence against the proposed meeting. When Nomura met with Hull on the evening of August 28 and began discussing detailed arrangements, Hull brought him up short by insisting that Japan would have to agree to nullify the Tripartite Pact and withdraw her troops from China before any conference between Konoye and Roosevelt could be held. Nomura indicated that the Tripartite Pact was not a major obstacle, but when he said that Japan could not easily compromise her interests in China, Hull made it unmistakably clear that "the China question was one of the pivotal questions underlying relations between the United States and Japan."[5] A week later, on September 3, President Roosevelt handed Nomura a note declaring that Japan would have to agree in advance to American principles of territorial integrity, commercial equality, and observance of the *status quo* in the Pacific. This note in effect ended any possibility of a summit conference. The United States was demanding that Japan give up her New Order in Asia as a precondition to meeting, while Konoye had promised the military leaders in Japan he would use the conference to secure American approval of Japanese dominance in the Far East.

Even before Roosevelt's discouraging note of September 3 reached Tokyo, the Japanese Army and Navy leaders had decided to invade the Dutch East Indies before the end of the year to secure desperately needed oil. The Army general staff

[4]*Ibid.*, pp. 572, 574–75.
[5]*Ibid.*, p. 578.

insisted that the war preparations would have to be put in motion by October; if diplomacy failed to restore normal trade
with the United States by that time, war would follow.

On September 3 Konoye accepted this proposed timetable,
still hopeful that he could negotiate a peaceful agreement with
the United States. Three days later an Imperial Conference
made the fateful decision "to proceed with war preparations so
that they be completed approximately toward the end of October." Meanwhile, Japan would seek to have England and the
United States agree to her "demands." "If, by the early part of
October," the conference agreed, "there is still no prospect of
being able to attain our demands, we shall immediately decide
to open hostilities against the United States, Great Britain,
and the Netherlands."[6] Japan was determined to carry out her
program in the Far East, by diplomacy if possible, by war if
necessary.

Throughout September Nomura attempted to secure Hull's
agreement to the Japanese demands in the Far East. Peace was
possible, the Japanese envoy argued, if only the United States
would end its economic sanctions, stop its aid to Chiang Kai-
shek, and permit Japan to liquidate the war in China. Although American military leaders pleaded with the administration to avoid a showdown in the Far East until American
strength in the Pacific could be increased, Hull and Roosevelt
agreed that the United States could not buy time by selling out
China. On October 2 Hull replied to Japan. In a long note he
reviewed the negotiations between the two countries and the
major point at issue. No meeting between Roosevelt and
Konoye could be held, Hull asserted, until Japan gave a
"clear-cut manifestation" of her intention to withdraw her
troops from China and Indo-China.[7] This rigid statement of
American policy ended the last chance for diplomatic accommodation between Japan and the United States in 1941.
Hull was asking Japan to give up all her hard-won gains of the
past decade — Manchuria, China, Indo-China — as well as the
prospects for acquiring control of all Southeast Asia, in return

[6]Robert J. C. Butow, *Tojo and the Coming of the War* (Princeton, 1961),
p. 250.

[7]*Foreign Relations: Japan, 1931–1941*, II, 660.

for American trade and friendship. The price was too high. Konoye had exhausted his alloted time for diplomacy; on October 16 his government fell from power, and General Hideki Tojo, leader of the army expansionists, formed a new cabinet pledged to fulfill Japan's destiny in Asia.

Historians have ever since asked whether a conference between Konoye and Roosevelt could have averted war. The consensus is that it would have failed. The two nations were on a collision course, and neither leader could compromise the vital interests of his country. Konoye could not forego Japan's New Order in Asia merely to placate the United States. Any such surrender would have been repudiated by the Japanese military leaders and would have cost Konoye his position and probably his life. Nor could Roosevelt permit Japan to subjugate China and dominate the Far East. Yet a more flexible and realistic American policy might have delayed a showdown with Japan. By meeting with Konoye and seeking a temporary *modus vivendi*, Roosevelt could have gained the time that American military leaders felt was essential to strengthen the defenses of the Philippines, Hawaii, and other American outposts in the Pacific. By standing firmly on principle, Roosevelt and Hull missed an opportunity to postpone the inevitable clash with Japan.

I

In the Atlantic as in the Far East, the United States moved inexorably toward war in the fall of 1941. The submarine menace eased somewhat in July and August following the American occupation of Iceland. Nine eastbound British convoys carried over 4 million tons of supplies across the North Atlantic during the summer, and not a single ship was lost. But in September the U-boats again found their targets. On September 8 twelve German submarines attacked a slow British convoy south of Iceland and over a three-day span sank 15 merchant ships. Britain had badly overtaxed her limited destroyer strength in escorting the heavy run of summer convoys, and the strain on ships and crews was reaching a critical point. Supply shipments to Russia, which had to go around the German-occupied coast of Norway to Murmansk, added a new and very heavy burden that Britain could not handle alone. Unless the United States Navy shared the escort duty, Great Britain would lose the Battle of the Atlantic by default.

Roosevelt, fully aware of the British plight, had promised at the Atlantic Conference that American naval units would escort convoys of British ships as far as Iceland. Yet despite this pledge, he held back, uncertain how he would justify such a policy to the American people. On September 1 Admiral Ernest King drew up an elaborate operation plan for convoy duty by the Atlantic fleet, but still Roosevelt hesitated. Then on September 4 Germany provided the pretext the President was seeking. The American destroyer *Greer*, carrying passengers and mail to Iceland, was attacked by a German submarine in the North Atlantic. The submarine fired two torpedoes; both missed the *Greer*, which responded with depth charges that also missed. Later reports revealed that the *Greer* had been trailing the submarine for over three hours in cooperation with a British patrol plane which dropped four depth charges on the U-boat. The submarine commander, far from being guilty of an unprovoked assault, had turned in desperation on his pursuer in an effort to escape destruction.

President Roosevelt, however, did not wait to ascertain the full story of the *Greer* episode. At a press conference on September 5 he called the attack deliberate. Later that day he met with Secretary of State Hull and Harry Hopkins and decided to institute the long-delayed convoys by the American Navy. He asked Hull to prepare a draft of a speech he would deliver to the American people about this momentous decision. When Hull cautiously sent in a weak statement, Hopkins and Judge Sam Rosenman, the President's chief speech writer, prepared a much stronger draft, which Roosevelt strengthened even more. On September 10 Roosevelt read the speech to Secretaries Hull, Knox and Stimson, who warmly endorsed it, and the next day he went over it with a bipartisan group of Congressional leaders.

Roosevelt delivered his address, one of the boldest speeches of his long career, to a nationwide radio audience on September 11. In blunt, biting phrases, he accused Germany of piracy in the *Greer* incident and called U-boats "the rattlesnakes of the Atlantic." Germany, he warned the nation, was seeking to secure control of the seas as a prelude to conquest of the Western Hemisphere. "This attack on the *Greer* was no localized military operation in the North Atlantic," declared Roosevelt. "This was one determined step towards creating a permanent world system based on force, terror, and murder." Therefore, the President continued, American ships would no longer wait to be attacked, implying, but not clearly stating, a new policy of shoot-on-sight for American destroyers. Then, in unambiguous language, he announced the beginning of American convoys: ". . . our patrolling vessels and planes will protect all merchant ships—not only American ships but ships of any flag—engaged in commerce in our defensive waters." "From now on," he concluded, "if German or Italian vessels of war enter the waters the protection of which is necessary for American defense they do so at their own peril."[8]

This "shoot-on-sight" speech, as it has been deceptively labeled by many historians, marked a decisive step toward war. Ever since the passage of the Lend-Lease Act in March, Winston Churchill, along with many of the President's own advisers, had been urging Roosevelt to insure the delivery of supplies by authorizing the United States Navy to undertake escort duty. Repeatedly, the President had given in to this pressure only to reverse himself on the grounds that the American people were not yet ready to face the risk of war involved in convoying. Now he had committed himself publicly.

Yet Roosevelt's boldness was misleading. Even in taking a momentous step, he acted deviously, seizing on a questionable incident and portraying it as a simple case of aggression, which it clearly was not. Roosevelt evidently still believed that he could not be honest with the American people. The public opinion polls, however, indicate that he seriously overestimated the strength of isolationism. Surveys in September showed that nearly 80% of the people opposed participation in the war; but such results were to be expected— rarely do

[8]Department of State, *Peace and War: United States Foreign Policy, 1931–1941* (Washington, 1943), pp. 741–42, 743.

people respond positively to a simple query about entering a major conflict. In early October, when George Gallup asked the more realistic question, Do you think it more important to defeat Hitler than to stay out of the war?, over 70% answered that it was better to insure defeat of Hitler. The American people wanted to stay at peace, but not at the cost of a German victory. Thus, to the President's relief, they responded enthusiastically to this convoy decision, taking in stride its risk of war. Indeed, the public reaction was so favorable that Roosevelt could have begun convoys months earlier with solid public support.

On September 16, five days after the President's speech, the first American-escorted convoy left the Canadian port of Halifax for the hazardous voyage across the Atlantic. Five United States Navy destroyers relieved the initial Canadian escort vessels south of Newfoundland on September 17. For a week fifty merchant ships lumbered through the Atlantic while the destroyers patrolled for submarines. On September 25, some five hundred miles south of Iceland, the American escort transferred the convoy to British units without incident. Roosevelt's estimate that Hitler wanted to avoid a showdown with the United States while he was engaged in the Russian campaign proved to be correct. When news of the President's September 11 speech reached Berlin, Admiral Raeder had prepared a long memorandum for Hitler setting forth the reasons why Germany would have to begin attacking American ships. The Nazi leader agreed with the arguments, but he insisted that submarine commanders must take care "to avoid any incidents in the war on merchant shipping before about the middle of October."[9] For the time being, at least, Germany would refrain from challenging the American Navy in the North Atlantic.

The next problem confronting Roosevelt was the prohibition on arming American merchant vessels and the ban on their entry into war zones contained in the 1939 Neutrality Act. With American cargo ships now traveling to Iceland to supply the American garrison there, it was essential that they

[9]Hans L. Trefousse, *Germany and American Neutrality, 1939–1941* (New York, 1951), pp. 120–21.

be permitted to carry deck guns for protection against surface attacks by German submarines. In addition, if the United States was fully committed to the policy of insuring the delivery of lend-lease supplies to Britain, it would be very helpful to have American ships carry these goods acro.˙ the Atlantic and thus relieve the over-burdened British mercha.. marine. When Roosevelt's advisers had pressed this question on him in July, he had consulted with Congressional leaders, and their negative reaction had caused him to defer the issue. Encouraged by the favorable response to his convoy speech, the President decided to ask for revision of the Neutrality Act. Yet again he acted with indirection. On October 9 Roosevelt asked Congress to repeal only Section VI of the Act, which prohibited the arming of merchant ships, a step he knew most Congressmen favored. Then, in less specific terms, he urged Congress to "give earnest and early attention" to other phases of the Neutrality Act. With studied vagueness, he suggested that Congress reconsider "keeping our ships out of the ports of our own friends," but he never specifically asked for repeal of the combat zone provisions of the Neutrality Act of 1939.[10]

The House of Representatives considered the President's ambiguous requests in late October. Fearful of defeat by the isolationists, Congressional leaders restricted the legislation to repeal of Section VI, and thus the issue was confined to arming American merchant ships. As the debate reached its climax, news arrived that a German submarine had topedoed an American destroyer, the *Kearney*, while it was attempting to beat off a wolfpack raid on a British convoy. The *Kearney* managed to limp back into Iceland, and the next day the House voted to arm American merchant ships by the impressive margin of 259 to 138. In the tally Democratic Representatives backed the administration overwhelmingly, while three out of every four Republicans voted no.

The attack on the *Kearney* and the vote in the House led to public demands that the Senate repeal the entire Neutrality Act. The administration, however, remained cautious, and finally decided to ask only that the Senate expand the legisla-

[10]Samuel Rosenman, ed., *The Public Papers and Addresses of Franklin D. Roosevelt* (13 vols.; New York, 1938-1950), X, 409.

tion to strike out the ban on American ships entering combat zones. Even this request caused a bitter debate in the Senate. The sinking of the American destroyer *Reuben James* with the loss of 115 lives on October 31 intensified the isolationist opposition, and lent support to the America First charge that Roosevelt was "asking Congress to issue an engraved drowning license to American seamen."[11] If Britain needed American ships, suggested the administration's opponents, why not give them to her under lend-lease and thus avoid risking American lives on the high seas? However, on November 7, the Senate voted 50 to 37 to permit the administration to arm American merchant ships and send them into the war zone. The bill was then referred back to the House, which concurred in the combat zone provision by 18 votes, 212 to 194.

The narrow margin by which Congress revised the Neutrality Act in November 1941 seemed to confirm Roosevelt's caution. Yet the vote did reflect the attitude of the American people. Many Congressmen voted against the administration to protest what they considered lax labor policies that were hampering the defense effort. Other Representatives and Senators, aware that the public favored revision, felt compelled to vote against a measure that might soon lead to a war which the people had repeatedly said they did not want to enter. Unable to reconcile the conflicting public desire to do everything possible to speed the defeat of Hitler yet remain at peace, these Congressmen decided to play it safe. Given the failure of the President to deal forthrightly with this contradiction in the public mood, their vote is understandable.

Despite the closeness of the vote, the meaning of the Congressional action was clear. The United States had finally abandoned the major portions of neutrality legislation adopted in the prewar years. The only meaningful restrictions left in force were the ban on American travel on belligerent ships and the prohibition on loans, which had long since been circumvented by the Lend-Lease Act. All that remained then was a hollow shell which stood as a monument to the naive belief of the American people in the mid 1930s that they could find safety

[11]Wayne S. Cole, *America First* (Madison, Wis., 1953), p. 163.

behind a legislative barricade when the world went to war. As long as it lasted intact, the Neutrality Act had served its purpose of keeping the nation out of war. But in the interval the American people had been taught by events overseas that the security of the nation, not avoidance of hostilities, was the true goal of American foreign policy.

The revision of the Neutrality Act, together with the even more important convoy decision, brought American policy in the Atlantic in line with the stand taken in Asia. In both regions the United States had exhausted the techniques of peaceful diplomacy and had challenged the Axis powers to a showdown. Just as Japan had to face the issue of peace or war over the freezing order of July 26, so Nazi Germany had to decide whether to accept the provocative American policy in the North Atlantic. In essence, Roosevelt surrendered the decision for war to Tojo and Hitler. It was now only a question of who would strike first.

II

In late October the new Tojo cabinet, instructed by the Emperor to examine afresh the diplomatic crisis with the United States, held a series of critical liason conferences with the Army and Navy chiefs. Tojo was not unalterably bent on war, but he was determined to end the months of indecision. Aware that the Navy alone was using up 400 tons of oil each hour, the militarists argued that Japan had to act immediately to create its New Order in Asia. For ten days they presented their case to the cabinet. In a meeting that began at 9 A.M. on November 1 and lasted into the early hours of the next morning, the Tojo government made its decision. Diplomacy would continue for another month, but if the United States had not resumed trade by midnight on November 30, Japan would go to war. "Rather than await extinction," wrote Prime Minister Tojo later, "it were better to face death by breaking through the encircling ring and find a way for existence."[12]

[12]William L. Langer and S. Everett Gleason, *The Undeclared War, 1940–1941* (New York, 1953), p. 852.

On November 5 the Japanese leaders held a conference before the Emperor to make the deliberations official. The Emperor listened silently while Tojo announced that Japan would present the United States with two proposals, Plan A and Plan B. Tojo contended that the United States, once it understood the determination of Japan, would give way, but if the Americans continued to hold out, on December 1, regardless of whatever progress had been made in the negotiations, Japan would declare war. There was no dissent. A few hours later the Supreme Command issued operational orders with the statement, "War with Netherlands, America, England inevitable; general operational preparations to be completed by early December."[13]

That same day, November 5, 1941, the Joint Board of the Army and Navy was meeting in Washington to advise the Roosevelt administration on the military position of the United States in the Far East. In late October Chiang Kai-shek had bombarded both President Roosevelt and Prime Minister Winston Churchill with urgent requests for aid against an expected Japanese assault on the Burma Road. Cordell Hull, fearful that any additional American move to aid China would lead to Japanese reprisal, wanted the views of the military leaders. In a long memorandum, the Joint Board, headed by Admiral Harold Stark and General George C. Marshall, urged caution. The military planners stressed the need for a defensive stance in the Far East while concentrating on the German menace in Europe. They advised against any plan to use American forces in China and they recommended that "no ultimatum be delivered to Japan." But most important, the military leaders did draw a line beyond which the United States could not allow Japan to go. They felt that any Japanese attack on American, British, or Dutch territory in Southeast Asia, or a movement beyond the 100th meridian in Thailand, would have to be met by "military action against Japan."[14]

---

[13]*Ibid.*, p. 854.

[14]*Hearings before the Joint Committee on the Investigation of the Pearl Harbor Attack*, 79th Congress, 1st and 2nd Session (39 parts; Washington, 1946), Part 14, p. 1062.

November 5 thus marks the beginning of the countdown for war in the Pacific. The United States would refrain from provocation in China, but if Japan attempted to expand into Southeast Asia, a military showdown would follow automatically. Both sides had taken stock of their goals and resources; both had set the conditions for maintaining peace. Roosevelt wondered what he should do if Japan bypassed American territory and struck only at British and Dutch possessions. At a cabinet meeting on November 7 Roosevelt put this question to his advisers, and they answered unanimously that in such a contingency the American people would undoubtedly back the administration and support a declaration of war against Japan. Although Roosevelt did not then officially adopt policies recommended by the Joint Board on November 5, they became by implication the American position. Japan could continue its conquest of China; any movement to the south meant war with the United States.

In the context of these military decisions the negotiations that continued throughout November were virtually without meaning. In an elaborate move to deceive the United States, Japan sent Saburo Kurusu, an experienced diplomat, to join Nomura in presenting Plans A and B to the United States. Kurusu made a dramatic flight by clipper across the Pacific, landing in San Francisco on November 14, where he told newsmen he had come to "break through the line and make a touchdown."[15] But he brought no new proposals with him. By the time he arrived in Washington, Hull had examined the first Japanese plan and rejected it. Familiar with the terms because of Magic, Hull had barely been able to wait a decent diplomatic interval to turn down a proposal which would give an American blessing to a Japanese-dominated Asia.

On November 20, Nomura and Kurusu presented Plan B, which was in the nature of a stop-gap agreement, designed to ease the current crisis between the two nations without grappling with the fundamental issues. In essence, Japan asked for a free hand in China and a resumption of trade with the United States, including a stated quantity of oil, promising in

[15]Langer and Gleason, *Undeclared War*, p. 869.

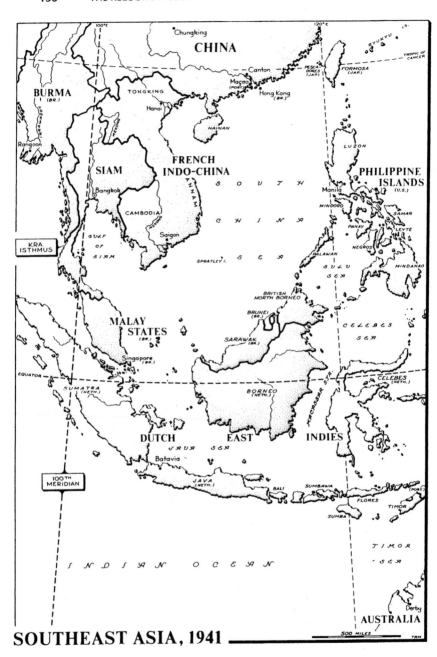

SOUTHEAST ASIA, 1941

return to withdraw her troops from southern Indo-China and pledging "not to make any armed advancement into any of the regions in the South-eastern Asia and the Southern Pacific area."[16] Given the previous American decision to write off China and to postpone war with Japan, the terms of Plan B offered some hope. Hull, aware that President Roosevelt favored a *modus vivendi* with Japan, had his subordinates in the State Department begin drafting a counter-proposal to submit to Nomura and Kurusu.

Two days later Cordell Hull called in the ambassadors of Britain, China, and the Netherlands to inform them of the terms of the American *modus vivendi*. It called for a 90-day truce in the Far East during which China and Japan would discuss "a peaceful settlement of their differences," Japan would withdraw its troops from southern Indo-China, and the United States would end its freezing order but maintain strict control over the export of critical materials to Japan.[17] Such a plan would meet the needs of the American military for time to shore up the defenses of American outposts in the Pacific, yet it would not prejudice the American diplomatic stand against new Japanese aggression. The *modus vivendi* was doomed from the outset. At the very time that Hull was presenting it to the ambassadors, Naval Intelligence was deciphering a note from the Japanese Foreign Office to Nomura and Kurusu. Replying to a plea of the envoys for more time, the Japanese government placed a deadline of November 29 for the signing of an agreement with the United States. After that, "things are automatically going to happen."[18] A sense of futility enveloped Cordell Hull as he went through the motions of preparing the *modus vivendi*. The proposal was designed purely to gain precious time for the American Army and Navy; the intercepted Japanese message clearly revealed that Japan would not tolerate further delay. On November 25 the friendly governments concerned sent in their appraisal of the plan. The Dutch were receptive, though somewhat skeptical; the British were very cool, but willing to follow American initia-

[16]*Foreign Relations: Japan, 1931–1941*, II, 755.
[17]*Pearl Harbor Attack*, Part 14, p. 1114.
[18]Feis, *Road to Pearl Harbor*, p. 313.

tive; the Chinese were unalterably opposed. Chiang Kai-shek instructed the Chinese ambassador in Washington to resist any deal with Japan. On November 26 a weary Cordell Hull informed President Roosevelt of the impasse, and the two men agreed to shelve the proposed *modus vivendi*.

On November 26 the United States government gave Japan a formal reply to Plan B. In a ten-point memorandum, Hull demanded that Japan withdraw all its troops from China and Indo-China and accept the promise of American trade and financial assistance as a substitute for the New Order in Asia. Certain that diplomacy had failed, Hull and Roosevelt were simply putting down their principles for posterity to examine. The next day, November 27, Admiral Stark and General Marshall sent war-warning messages to their commanders in the Pacific.

III

The American ten-point note arrived in Tokyo on November 27. At a Liaison Conference later that day, the Japanese leaders denounced the proposal as a humiliating ultimatum which was totally unacceptable. They then decided to carry out their resolve of early November and proceed with the preparations for war. On December 1 an Imperial Conference was held to ratify the decision. Tojo opened the brief ceremony by summing up the impasse between the United States and Japan. ". . . it is now utterly impossible for Japan to permit the present situation to continue any longer, he declared. "In such circumstances, Japan has now no other way than to wage war against the United States, Britain and the Netherlands in order to achieve a solution of the present critical situation and to secure its existence and self-defense."[19] For two hours other cabinet members echoed Tojo's theme of war or defeat. Then the Emperor, ever the silent listener, left the chamber. Japan had decided on war.

In Washington the intercepted Japanese messages did not reveal the decision reached in Tokyo, but the evidence all

[19]Langer and Gleason, *Undeclared War*, p. 910.

pointed inescapably in that direction. President Roosevelt spent the weekend of November 29-30 at Warm Springs, Georgia, but hastened back to the capital on December 1. Both Secretary Hull and Admiral Stark warned him of the impending hostilities. Before leaving on his weekend trip, the President had asked the State Department to draft a personal letter to the Emperor as well as a message to Congress alerting the nation to the imminence of war. Hull now persuaded Roosevelt to shelve both of these approaches, and instead wait for more specific evidence of Japanese aggression.

The President's greatest fear during this first week of December was a Japanese thrust in Southeast Asia that would bypass American territory. Reports came in of massive Japanese troop movements in Indo-China that seemed to be a prelude to a strike at Thailand, Malaya, and the Dutch East Indies. On November 30 Winston Churchill sent Roosevelt a cable asking him to warn Japan that any further step in Southeast Asia would compel him "to place the gravest issues before Congress."[20] Roosevelt could not go this far, but he instructed the State Department to ask the Japanese government for a statement of intentions regarding troop concentrations in Indo-China. On the afternoon of December 1, Lord Halifax, the British Ambassador, called on the President to press personally the points that Churchill had raised. Halifax told Roosevelt that England expected the Japanese to invade Thailand, and that the British were planning to move into the Kra Isthmus of that country in order to prevent its seizure. The President replied that if Japan attacked British or Dutch territory, "we should obviously all be together." Moreover, Britain could count on American support if her occupation of the Kra Isthmus led to hostilities with Japan, though it might be a few days before such support would be forthcoming. Two days later, at another conference with Halifax, Roosevelt became more specific, stating that he would extend "armed support" to Britain in case of a Japanese attack.[21] On December 4 Lord Halifax expressed to the President the "very deep apprecia-

[20]Winston S. Churchill, *The Grand Alliance* (Boston, 1950), p. 599.

[21]Sir Llewellyn Woodward, *British Foreign Policy in the Second World War* (London, 1962), pp. 186-87.

tion" of his government.[22] Since the summer of 1941 Churchill
had been pressing for a guarantee that the United States
would fight if Japan invaded British and Dutch territory in
Southeast Asia. Although his own Army and Navy Joint Board
had recommended such a step in early November, Roosevelt
had consistently avoided a binding commitment. Thus, in
pledging armed support, Roosevelt revealed his personal
belief, supported by the opinions of his cabinet members, that
Congress would declare war even if the Japanese sweep
through Southeast Asia bypassed American territory.[23]

As the week progressed, the situation steadily deteriorated.
On December 5 the Japanese replied to the inquiry about the
build-up of troops in Indo-China, claiming it was directed
solely against China. Then on December 6 the British government reported that two large Japanese convoys, accompanied
by major units of the fleet, were round the southern tip of
Indo-China on their way either to Thailand or Malaya. Realizing that the climax was approaching, Roosevelt sought desperately for some way to regain the initiative. He turned finally to the idea of a personal message to Emperor Hirohito
pleading for peace. The State Department worked feverishly
through the afternoon and early evening of Saturday,
December 6, on the proposed message to the Emperor. One
draft consisted of a simplified *modus vivendi* proposal, suggesting that for ninety days the United States and Japan
refrain from any movement or use of armed force in the
Pacific. Roosevelt rejected this draft in favor of a brief
message which dwelt on the Japanese build-up of troops in
Indo-China, which he termed "a keg of dynamite." Roosevelt
asked the Emperor to undertake the withdrawal of these
forces. "I am confident that both of us," the President stated,
"for the sake of the peoples not only of our own great countries
but for the sake of humanity in neighboring territories, have a
sacred duty to restore traditional amity and prevent further
death and destruction in the world."[24]

[22]*Ibid.*, p. 187.

[23]For a clear analysis of this critical point, see Raymond A. Esthus, "President Roosevelt's Commitment to Britain to Intervene in a Pacific War,"
Mississippi Valley Historical Review, L (June, 1963), 34-38.

[24]*Foreign Relations: Japan, 1931-1941*, II, 786.

The State Department dispatched this urgent message at 9 P.M., December 6, instructing Ambassador Grew to deliver it as soon as possible. At the same time, the long-awaited Japanese reply to the ten-part American note of November 26 was coming in over the cables. The first thirteen parts of a fourteen-part message were deciphered almost simultaneously in the Japanese Embassy and in the offices of U.S. Naval Intelligence. The message consisted of a tedious review of Japanese-American relations and a verbose analysis of the American note of November 26. More ominous was the instruction to Nomura and Kurusu not to present the message to the State Department until the fourteenth part arrived the next day, December 7. Copies of the Japanese message were handed to State Department officials and the President during the evening. According to the naval officer who delivered the message to the White House, the President read through the dispatch and then turned to Harry Hopkins and said, "This means war."[25] Nevertheless, no further action was taken that evening. The next morning the fourteenth part of the Japanese note arrived. Charging that the United States was conspiring with Britain to block the New Order in Asia, the message concluded, "The Japanese Government regrets to have to notify hereby the American Government that in view of the attitude of the American Government it cannot but consider that it is impossible to reach an agreement through further negotiations."[26]

The intercepted Japanese message indicated clearly that Japan was severing diplomatic relations and planning on war. But the precise place where the first blow would fall remained unknown. In the Pentagon General Marshall belatedly prepared an additional warning message to American commanders in the Pacific. At the State Department Hull learned that Nomura and Kurusu had asked for an audience at 1 P.M. to deliver the fourteen-point message. At the White House Roosevelt met with Hu Shih, the Chinese ambassador, and read him the text of his personal appeal to the Emperor. "This is my last effort at peace," Roosevelt told Hu Shih. "I am

[25]*Pearl Harbor Attack*, Part 10, p. 4662.
[26]*Foreign Relations: Japan, 1931–1941*, II, 792.

afraid it may fail." Then the President voiced his fear that
Japan would try "foul play," saying that something "nasty"
might take place within the next 48 hours in Thailand, Malaya, the East Indies, or "possibly" the Philippines.[27]

At the very time that Roosevelt was speaking, a Japanese
task force had launched its planes for a devastating raid on the
American Pacific Fleet at Pearl Harbor. The Japanese ships
had left the Kurile Islands on November 25 and had passed
unnoticed through the icy waters of the North Pacific. Japan
could have recalled this striking force if the United States had
made a sudden diplomatic surrender; instead, it was ordered
to fulfill its mission. By knocking out the American fleet,
Japan could safely carry out her major thrust into Southeast
Asia and the Philippines.

When Nomura and Kurusu arrived an hour late at the State
Department to deliver the last note, Hull already knew of the
attack on Pearl Harbor. He pretended to read the message
that the two envoys handed him; he already knew its contents
and significance. Then, unable to repress his fury any longer,
the Secretary denounced the Japanese government in scathing
language and dismissed the envoys.

Throughout the afternoon reports came in to the President
and his advisers. The Pacific fleet at Pearl Harbor was crippled; 2400 Americans had lost their lives. For years afterward
investigating committees would sift through the voluminous
evidence in the search for scapegoats for this national tragedy.
At the time, however, there was a sense of release, if not relief.
When Roosevelt summoned his advisers to a late afternoon
conference, Harry Hopkins recorded the mood they shared.
"The conference met in not too tense an atmosphere because I
think that all of us believed that in the last analysis the enemy
was Hitler and that he could never be defeated without force
of arms; that sooner or later we were bound to be in the war
and that Japan had given us an opportunity."[28]

One critical question still remained unanswered—did war
with Japan mean war with Germany as well? When Roosevelt
read a draft of a message to Congress calling for war with

[27]Feis, *Road to Pearl Harbor*, p. 340.
[28]Robert Sherwood, *Roosevelt and Hopkins* (New York, 1948), p. 431.

Japan, Secretary Stimson objected. "I pointed out," Stimson recorded in his diary, "that we knew . . . that Germany had pushed Japan into this and that we should ask for a declaration of war against Germany also."[29] No one supported this suggestion. The next day President Roosevelt delivered a brief message to Congress. Declaring that December 7 was "a date which will live in infamy," Roosevelt presented a simple resume of the Japanese attacks in Hawaii, the Philippines and Southeast Asia, and asked Congress to recognize that a state of war existed between the United States and Japan.[30] With only one dissenting vote, Congress complied.

Hitler resolved the dilemma over war in the Atlantic. Although uninformed by the Japanese in advance, Hitler was pleased with the strike at Pearl Harbor. On December 11 the German Foreign Office handed a note to the American Chargé d'Affaires in Berlin severing diplomatic relations and declaring war. There was no mention of Japan. Instead, Germany stated that "the Government of the United States from initial violations of neutrality had finally proceeded to open acts of war against Germany."[31] In short, Germany was masquerading as the defender of international law self-righteously fighting against American encroachments. Later the same day Roosevelt willingly faced the Nazi challenge: "The forces endeavoring to enslave the entire world are moving towards this hemisphere," he proclaimed to Congress.[32] Virtually without debate Congress unanimously passed a Joint Resolution affirming a state of war with Germany.

Thus to the very end, the pattern of American reaction to events abroad held true. From the first signs of aggression in the 1930s to the attack on Pearl Harbor, the United States refused to act until there was no other choice. The American people believed in the 1930s that they could escape the contagion of war. When the fall of France destroyed this illusion, they embraced the comforting notion that through material aid they could defeat Hitler without entering the conflict.

[29]Langer and Gleason, *Undeclared War*, p. 938.
[30]State Department, *Peace and War*, p. 839.
[31]Langer and Gleason, *Undeclared War*, p. 940.
[32]State Department, *Peace and War*, p. 849.

When Japan threatened all Asia, Americans naively believed that economic pressure would compel her to retreat. Even when Japan responded with the attack on Pearl Harbor, the United States ignored the Axis alliance and waited for Hitler to force America into the European war.

American foreign policy proved disappointing in a period of grave international disorder. Neither the President nor the people faced up to the peril posed by the Axis powers until the danger became all too real. The latent power of the nation remained untapped; the strongest country in the world refrained from using its influence to halt the spread of aggression in Europe and Asia. By surrendering the initiative to Germany and Japan, the United States made itself the prisoner of events abroad. The Japanese attack finally forced the nation to end its indecision and begin the long and costly struggle to defeat the Axis threat to American security.

SUGGESTIONS FOR FURTHER READING

The best introduction to the literature on American entry into World War II is Robert Dallek, *Franklin D. Roosevelt and American Foreign Policy, 1932–1945* (New York, 1979). Dallek views FDR as a realistic statesman who moderated his policies in response to domestic pressures. The most comprehensive and wide-ranging account of American diplomacy from 1937 to 1941 is the two-volume study by William L. Langer and S. Everett Gleason, *The Challenge to Isolation, 1937–1940* (New York, 1952) and *The Undeclared War, 1940–1941* (New York, 1953). Donald F. Drummond, *The Passing of American Neutrality, 1937–1941* (Ann Arbor, Mich., 1955) is a more compact survey of the same period. Lloyd C. Gardner, *Economic Aspects of New Deal Diplomacy* (Madison, Wis., 1964) is a provocative analysis of Roosevelt's foreign policy. Joseph P. Lash has written a warmly sympathetic account of the close ties between the American and British leaders in *Roosevelt and Churchill, 1939–1941: The Partnership That Saved the West* (New York, 1976). The best book on Roosevelt's role as wartime leader is James MacGregor Burns, *Roosevelt: The Soldier of Freedom* (New York, 1970). Three general surveys, Selig Adler, *The Uncertain Giant, 1921–1941* (New York, 1965), John E. Wiltz, *From Isolation to War, 1931–1941* (New York, 1968) and Arnold A. Offner, *The Origins of the Second World War* (New York, 1975), supersede such earlier accounts as Allan Nevins, *The New Deal and World Affairs* (New Haven, Conn., 1950) and Dexter Perkins, *The New Age of Franklin D. Roosevelt* (Chicago, 1956).

In the years immediately following the end of the Second World War, a group of historians, most of whom had strongly opposed entry into the war, published a series of books highly critical of President Roosevelt's policies. Charles A. Beard began the revisionist assault with *American Foreign Policy in the Making, 1932–1940* (New Haven, Conn., 1946) and *Presi-*

dent Roosevelt and the Coming of War, 1941 (New Haven, Conn., 1948), charging that Roosevelt had deceived the American people by talking peace while conspiring for war. Charles C. Tansill reiterated this theme, with more documentary evidence but even less logic, in *Back Door to War: The Roosevelt Foreign Policy, 1933–1941* (Chicago, 1952). Other revisionists accounts written in the early postwar years include William H. Chamberlin, *America's Second Crusade* (Chicago, 1930), Frederic S. Sanborn, *Design for War: A Study of Secret Power Politics, 1937–1941* (New York, 1951) and Harry Elmer Barnes, ed., *Perpetual War for Perpetual Peace* (Caldwell, Idaho, 1953), a collection of essays. These bitter attacks led Basil Rauch to write *Roosevelt: From Munich to Pearl Harbor* (New York, 1950), in which the author considerably overstates the case in defending Roosevelt.

Two recent books offer a more sophisticated revisionist analysis. Bruce Russett, writing from a post-Vietnam perspective, challenges the prevailing justification for American entry into World War II in *No Clear and Present Danger* (New York, 1972). The essays in Leonard P. Liggio and James J. Martin, eds., *Watershed of Empire: Essays on New Deal Foreign Policy* (Colorado Springs, 1976) are uniformly critical of FDR's conduct of diplomacy.

There is a wealth of memoirs and biographies which give insight into the development of American foreign policy in this period. In his classic *Roosevelt and Hopkins* (New York, 1948), Robert Sherwood provides a sympathetic portrait of Roosevelt's ideas and policies. My essays in *Roosevelt and World War II* (Baltimore, 1969) give a more critical view. For FDR's correspondence with his ambassadors during his first term in office, see Edgar B. Nixon, ed. *Franklin D. Roosevelt and Foreign Affairs, 1933–1937* (3 vols.; Cambridge, Mass., 1969). *The Memoirs of Cordell Hull* (2 vols; New York, 1948) are very full, but the Secretary of State often overstated his role in American diplomacy. Julius W. Pratt gives a thorough account of Hull's diplomacy in *Cordell Hull, 1933–1944 (American Secretaries of State and Their Diplomacy*, Volumes XII and XIII, New York, 1964). The views of Secretary of War Stimson are assessed in Henry L. Stimson and Mc-

George Bundy, *On Active Service in Peace and War* (New York, 1948), frankly defensive; in Richard N. Current, *Secretary Stimson: A Study in Statecraft* (New Brunswick, N.J., 1954), acidly critical; and in Elting E. Morison, *Turmoil and Tradition: A Study of the Life and Times of Henry L. Stimson* (Boston, 1960), openly sympathetic. Two books by Sumner Welles, *The Time for Decision* (New York, 1944) and *Seven Decisions That Shaped History* (New York, 1951) as well as two volumes of John M. Blum's *From the Morgenthau Diaries, Years of Crisis, 1928–1938* (Boston, 1959) and *Years of Urgency, 1938–1941* (Boston, 1965) give insight into a pair of key figures of the Roosevelt administration. For a glimpse into the workings of the State Department, see Nancy Harvison Hooker, ed., *The Moffat Papers: Selections from the Diplomatic Journals of Jay Pierrepont Moffat, 1919–1943* (Cambridge, Mass., 1956) and Beatrice Bishop Berle and Travis Beal Jacobs, *Navigating the Rapids, 1918–1971: From the Papers of Adolf A. Berle* (New York, 1973). The role of the military can be seen in Forrest C. Pogue, *George C. Marshall: Ordeal and Hope, 1939–1943* (New York, 1966).

Most general accounts of American entry into the Second World War neglect the period before 1937, when isolationism was strong enough to exert a powerful influence on American foreign policy. Selig Adler, *The Isolationist Impulse* (New York, 1957) is the best study of isolationism in the twentieth century, but it is sketchy on the 1930s. Manfred Jonas has written the most perceptive analysis of this phenomenon in *Isolationism in America, 1935–1941* (Ithaca, N.Y., 1966). For other views of isolationism in the 1930s, see Leroy N. Rieselbach, *The Roots of Isolationism* (Indianapolis, Ind., 1966) and the essays in Alexander DeConde, ed., *Isolation and Security* (Durham, N.C., 1957). Justin D. Doenecke gives a thorough bibliographic analysis in *The Literature of Isolationism: A Guide to Non–Interventionist Scholarship, 1930–1972* (Colorado Springs, 1972). The best studies of pacifism in this period are John K. Nelson, *The Peace Prophets* (Chapel Hill, N.C., 1967), which stresses pacifist thought, and Charles Chatfield, *For Peace and Justice: Pacifism in America, 1914–1941* (Knoxville, Tenn., 1971), which traces the political activities of peace advocates. James J. Martin criticizes the shift in liberal thought from pacifism to interventionism in *American Liberalism and World Politics, 1931–1941* (2 vols.; New York, 1964).

My own study, *The Illusion of Neutrality* (Chicago, 1962), focuses on the neutrality legislation of the 1930s. The role of Senator Nye is traced in Wayne S. Cole, *Senator Gerald P. Nye and American Foreign Relations* (Minneapolis, 1962), a sympathetic biography, and in John E. Wiltz, *In Search of Peace* (Baton Rouge, La., 1963) a careful analysis of the munitions investigation. Fred L. Israel sketches a critical portrait of the author of the neutrality acts in *Nevada's Key Pittman* (Lincoln, Neb., 1963). Richard P. Traina, *American Diplomacy and the Spanish Civil War* (Bloomington, Ind., 1968) supersedes the older study by F. Jay Taylor, *The United States and the Spanish Civil War* (New York, 1956) on administration policy toward the civil war in Spain, while Allen Guttmann, *The Wound in the Heart* (New York, 1962) examines the passionate response of the American people to this conflict.

The best study of American policy toward Germany in the 1930s is Arnold A. Offner, *American Appeasement* (Cambridge, Mass., 1969). Robert Dallek's biography, *Democrat and Diplomat: The life of William E. Dodd* (New York, 1968), traces the career of Roosevelt's ambassador to Germany. For American policy toward the Italian invasion of Ethiopia, see Brice Harris, Jr., *The United States and the Italo–Ethiopian Crisis* (Stanford, Cal., 1964).

A.J.P. Taylor has written the most provocative account of the events leading to war in Europe in *The Origins of the Second World War* (London, 1961) in which he argues that it was the blundering policy of appeasement pursued by England and France, not any prearranged policy by Hitler, which plunged Europe into war. Lawrence Lafore provides a more orthodox view in *The End of Glory: An Interpretation of the Origins of World War II* (Philadelphia, 1970). The official English view is given by Winston Churchill in the opening volume of *The Second World War* (6 vols.; Boston, 1948-53) and by Sir Llewellyn Woodward in *British Foreign Policy in the Second World War* (London, 1962). Books on American policy toward the European democracies include John McVickar Haight, Jr., *American Aid to France, 1938–1940* (New York, 1970), Warren F. Kimball, *The Most Unsordid Act: Lend–Lease, 1939–1941* (Baltimore, 1969), and Philip Goodhart, *Fifty Ships That Saved the World* (London, 1965), an account of the destroyers-for-bases deal. Hans L. Trefousse, *Germany and American Neutrality, 1939–1941* (New York, 1951), James V. Compton, *The Swastika and the Eagle* (Boston, 1967), Saul Friedlander, *Prelude to Downfall: Hitler and the United States, 1939–1941* (New York, 1967), and Alton Frye, *Nazi Germany and the American Hemisphere, 1939–1941* (New Haven, 1967) all deal with aspects of American relations with Germany during the first two years of the European war. For relations with the Soviet Union, see Robert Sobel, *The Origins of Interventionism: The United States and the Russo-Finnish War* (New York, 1960), Andrew J. Schwartz, *America and the Russo-Finnish War* (Washington, 1960) and Raymond H. Dawson, *The Decision to Aid Russia, 1941* (Chapel Hill, N.C., 1959), an excellent study.

Two contemporary accounts by journalists, Joseph Alsop and Robert Kintner, *American White Paper* (New York, 1940) and Forrest Davis and Ernest K. Lindley, *How War Came* (New York, 1942), capture the sense of crisis and urgency which characterized the period. Wayne S. Cole gives a perceptive and detached analysis of the major isolationist pressure group in *America First: The Battle Against Intervention, 1940–1941* (Madison, Wis., 1953); Walter Johnson provides a highly partisan account of the White Committee in *The Battle Against Isolation* (Chicago, 1944). Charles Lindbergh's role in the antiwar movement can be seen in *The Wartime Journals of Charles A. Lindbergh* (New York, 1970) and in Wayne S. Cole, *Charles A. Lindbergh and the Battle Against American Intervention in World War II* (New York, 1974). Michele Flynn Stenehjem traces the activities of another prominent isolationist in *An American First: John T. Flynn and the America First Committee* (New Rochelle, N.Y., 1976). Mark Lincoln Chadwin describes the more advanced interventionist movement in *The Hawks of World War II*

(Chapel Hill, N.C., 1974). For a favorable view of Roosevelt's leadership on entry into the war, see Gloria J. Barron, *Leadership in Crisis* (Port Washington, N.Y., 1973). Patrick Abbazia describes the battle of the Atlantic in *Mr. Roosevelt's Navy: The Private War of the U.S. Atlantic Fleet, 1939–1942* (Annapolis, 1975), while Theodore A. Wilson deals thoroughly with the Atlantic conference in *The First Summit* (Boston, 1969). Two volumes in the official military and naval histories of the war, Mark S. Watson, *Chief of Staff: PreWar Plans and Preparations* (Washington, 1950) and Samuel Eliot Morison, *The Battle of the Atlantic, September 1939–May 1943* (Boston, 1947), provide a wealth of material on strategy and foreign policy. James R. Leutze describes the staff conversations between British and American naval officers in *Bargaining for Supremacy: Anglo-American Naval Collaboration, 1937–1941* (Chapel Hill, N.C., 1977).

Several recent books deal with aspects of public opinion and the coming of war: David H. Culbert describes the roles of six radio commentators in *News for Everyone: Radio and Foreign Policy in Thirties America* (Westport, Conn., 1976); Michael Leigh analyzes the interaction between public attitudes and government policy in *Mobilizing Consent: Public Opinion and American Foreign Policy, 1937–1947* (Westport, Conn., 1976); George Q. Flynn examines Catholic attitudes in *Roosevelt and Romanism: Catholics and American Diplomacy, 1937–1945* (Westport, Conn., 1976); Jerome E. Edward traces the impact of a leading isolationist newspaper in *The Foreign Policy of Col. McCormick's Tribune, 1929–1941* (Reno, Nev., 1971).

The best single volume on the coming of war in the Pacific is still Herbert Feis, *The Road to Pearl Harbor* (Princeton, N.J., 1962), but see also the essays by Japanese and American historians in Dorothy Borg and Shumpei Okamoto, eds., *Pearl Harbor as History: Japanese–American Relations, 1931–1941* (New York, 1973). Japanese aggression is traced in F.C. Jones, *Japan's New Order in East Asia: Its Rise and Fall, 1937–1945* (London, 1954) and in David J. Lu, *From the Marco Polo Bridge to Pearl Harbor* (Washington, 1961). In *Tojo and the Coming of the War* (Stanford, Cal., 1961), Robert J.C. Butow provides a detailed and unsympathetic analysis of Japanese foreign policy. The same author describes the failure of an informal peace effort in *The John Doe Associates: Backdoor Diplomacy for Peace, 1941* (Stanford, Cal., 1974), while Nobutaka Ike has edited the records of the 1941 policy conferences of the Japanese leaders in *Japan's Decision for War* (Stanford, Cal., 1967).

Dorothy Borg focuses on American policy in her detailed study, *The United States and the Far Eastern Crisis, 1933–1938* (Cambridge, Mass., 1964); Stephen E. Pelz stresses the aggressive stand of the Japanese Navy in *Race to Pearl Harbor: The Failure of the Second London Naval Conference and the Onset of World War II* (Cambridge, Mass., 1974). Other books on the naval rivalry between the United States and Japan are Samuel Eliot Morison, *The Rising Sun in the Pacific, 1931–April, 1942* (Boston, 1948); James H. Herzog, *Closing the Open Door: American–Japanese Diplomatic Negotiations, 1936–1941* (Annapolis, 1973); and George C. Dyer, ed., *On the Treadmill to Pearl Harbor: The Memoirs of Admiral James O. Richardson* (Washington, 1973).

The most penetrating critique of the Roosevelt administration's Far Eastern policy is Paul Schroeder, *The Axis Alliance and Japanese-American Relations, 1941* (Ithaca, N.Y., 1958). Schroeder stresses the inflexible nature of the stand Roosevelt and Hull adopted toward Japan in the year before Pearl Harbor. A recent study of the role of a private American oil company, Irving H. Anderson, Jr., *The Standard-Vacuum Oil Company and United States East Asian Policy, 1933–1941* (Princeton, N.J., 1975), illuminates the importance of petroleum in the 1941 showdown with Japan. Two biographies, Waldo H. Heinrichs, Jr., *American Ambassador: Joseph C. Grew and the Development of the United States Diplomatic Tradition* (Boston, 1966) and Russell D. Buhite, *Nelson T. Johnson and American Policy toward China, 1925–1941* (East Lansing, Mich., 1968), provide information on the American envoys to Japan and China in the years before World War II.

The tragedy of Pearl Harbor has evoked an outpouring of books, though very few are of lasting value. The revisionists have combed through the voluminous evidence unearthed by various government investigating committees to document their extreme charges that President Roosevelt deliberately exposed the American fleet to destruction. George Morgenstern, *Pearl Harbor: The Story of the Secret War* (New York, 1947) and Robert A. Theobald, *The Final Secret of Pearl Harbor* (New York, 1954) are representative of this literature. Walter Millis, *This is Pearl* (New York, 1947), reflects the administration's early effort to place all the blame for the disaster on the commanders in Hawaii. By far the soundest account of Pearl Harbor, and the only one that seeks to explain what happened without issuing indictments, is Roberta Wohlstetter, *Pearl Harbor: Warning and Decision* (Stanford, Cal., 1962). Mrs. Wohlstetter realistically documents the intelligence failure and points out with frightening clarity the possibility of a similar lapse in the nuclear age. Ladislas Farago is more critical of the administration's intelligence efforts in *The Broken Seal* (New York, 1967). Martin Melosi traces the subsequent investigations of the tragedy and the political recriminations in *The Shadow of Pearl Harbor* (College Station, Tex., 1977).

Index

Garner, Vice President John Nance, 10, 66, 74, 75
Geneva General Disarmament Conference, 5, 6, 14
George, Senator Walter F., 65-66
George VI, King of England, 64, 94
Germany, 1, 11, 41, 47, 51: Czechoslovakia, 54-58; Ethiopian crisis, 16; neutrality legislation, 37, 40, 63; Rhineland reoccupation, 30-32; in World War II, 67ff
Gillette, Senator Guy M., 65-66
Goering, Marshal Harmann, 14
Good neighbor policy, 1-2, 49
Great Britain, 1, 43, 46, 50-51: Czechoslovakian crisis, 54-59; disarmament, 5-7, 14-15; Ethiopian crisis, 16, 27-28; neutrality legislation, 37, 39-40; Rhineland reoccupation, 28-30; Spanish Civil War, 31-34; in World War II, 67ff
Greater East Asia Co-Prosperity Sphere, 97, 124
Greece, 108, 117, 127
Greenland, 115-117
Greer, U.S.S., 148-149
Grew, Joseph C., 85, 100, 127, 144, 161

Halifax, Lord, 107, 154
Hawaiian Islands, 98, 135, 143, 147, 162-163
Hirohito, Emperor, 124, 154, 158, 160, 161
Hitler, Adolf, 2, 9, 47, 50: Czechoslovakian crisis, 53-58; disarmament, 13-15; Rhineland reoccupation, 30-31; in World War II, 67ff
Hoare, Sir Samuel, 16, 27
Hoare-Laval plan, 27
Hong Kong, 72
Hood, H. M. S., 118
Hoover Herbert, 4, 8, 72, 82
Hopkins, Harry L., 108, 114, 134, 148, 161, 162
House, Colonel Edward M., 11, 48
House Foreign Affairs Committee, 63-64
Hull, Cordell, 5, 7-8, 30, 36, 52, 80, 83, 95, 133, 139, 140, 155: Ethiopian crisis, 24-28; Manchurian crisis, 3-4;

negotiates with Nomura, 121-123, 143-145, 155-158; neutrality legislation, 18-20, 23, 62-67; opposes Welles plan, 49-51; sanctions on Japan, 98-101, 120, 124-127, 142; Sino-Japanese War, 43-45, 84-86; sketch of, 3-4
Hu Shih, 161

Iceland, 117, 132-133, 135, 148, 151
Ickes, Harold L., 82, 124
Indo-China, 97, 100, 119, 123-126, 138, 145-146, 159-160
Internationalists, 3, 32, 34, 82, 106, 118: advocate collective security, 11-13, 16-18; attitude toward Soviet Union, 129-131; destroyers-for-bases deal, 94-95; favor neutrality revision, 60-61; oppose neutrality legislation, 20, 22, 39-40
International Ladies Garment Workers Union, 91
International organization, 140-141
Isolationists, 2, 4, 31, 44, 59, 110: America First, 103-104; Atlantic Charter, 141; attitude toward Soviet Union, 82, 131; convoy issue, 113-114, 117; criticize Quarantine speech, 48-49; destroyers-for-bases deal, 93-96; favor Ludlow referendum, 48-49; favor neutrality legislation, 17-21, 28-29, 38, 62-65, 72-75, 77; oppose collective security, 7-10, 13; Selective Service, 136-137; Spanish Civil War, 34-35
Italy, 5, 29, 50, 51: Ethiopian crisis, 15-16, 23-27; Spanish Civil War, 33, 47; in World War II, 88ff
Iwakuro, Colonel Hideo, 121

Japan, 1, 2, 40, 51, 53, 106, 112, 137: aggressive policy in Asia, 96-102; Atlantic Conference, 138-139; attacks Pearl Harbor, 162-164; crisis with U.S., 142-147, 153-162; Manchurian crisis, 2, 9; trade embargoes, 118-120, 124-127; at war with China, 41-47, 84-85
Johnson, Senator Hiram, 7-8, 38-39
Johnson Act, 8